# Pen Turner's
# WORKBOOK

**3rd Edition** | **REVISED & EXPANDED**

3rd Edition | REVISED & EXPANDED

# Pen Turner's

# WORKBOOK

## MAKING PENS FROM SIMPLE TO STUNNING

Barry Gross

FOX CHAPEL
PUBLISHING

**Acknowledgments**

You hear horror stories of deadlines and editors that are demanding— maybe that is the way it is with other publishers, but the organization that Alan Giagnocavo has assembled is top shelf. From my editors John Kelsey, Paul Hambke, and Peg Couch, to Paul McGahren and his sales team, the "family" at Fox Chapel makes it a pleasure to write books for them. I want to thank them for putting up with my hectic schedule and working around my needs.

This is the third book I have written for Fox Chapel, and my friend Ed Ryan continues to be my mentor through this process. Ed is still unselfishly teaching students turning, and his "ABC's of tool techniques" is still the gold standard for students learning to turn. I want to thank Ed for showing me this technique and allowing me to pass it on to all of you.
— Barry Gross

Cover Photography: Scott Kriner
Gallery Photography: Scott Kriner and Greg Heisey
Interior Photography: Barry and Lenora Gross, and Scott Kriner

ISBN: 978–1–56523–763–6

Publisher's Cataloging-in-Publication Data

Gross, Barry.
    Pen turner's workbook / Barry Gross. -- 3rd edition, revised & expanded.
      pages cm
    Includes index.
    Summary: "Learn to make pens that are both practical - and beautiful! In this newly revised edition, author and expert pen turner, Barry Gross provides new pen kits and mechanisms with up-to-date techniques, along with the in-dept instruction and creative ideas for both the novice and the experiences turner looking for new ideas. From choosing a lathe to pen turning basics and even marketing your work—no detail has been left out! Also included is a section on casting your own acrylic pen bodies, so you can customize by embedding your own artwork and memorabilia. Instructions for turning pens made from Corian(r), InLace, antler and other materials included. "-- Provided by publisher.
    ISBN 978-1-56523-763-6 (pbk.)
    1. Turning (Lathe work) 2. Pens. I. Title.
 TT201.G755 2012
 684'.083--dc23
                          2012028205

To learn more about the other great books from Fox Chapel Publishing, or to find a retailer near you, call toll-free 800-457-9112 or visit us at *www.FoxChapelPublishing.com*.

**Note to Authors:** We are always looking for talented authors to write new books. Please send a brief letter describing your idea to Acquisition Editor, 1970 Broad Street, East Petersburg, PA 17520.

Printed in China
First printing

## Dedication

This book is dedicated to my best friend in life, my partner, my wife, Lenora, who always keeps encouraging and inspiring me to reach higher while never looking back! Analogous to the tree above with deep roots she keeps me grounded and without her unwavering support, this fifth book would not be possible.

# Contents

# Introduction

## Creating your own masterpiece pen!

Since 2003 when the first *Pen Turner's Workbook* was published, tens of thousands of pen turners have used my books as a reference guide to learn to turn pens. Some of you have created them for fun, others to earn extra income. No matter what your reasoning, you have turned to the *Pen Turner's Workbook* and I want to personally thank you.

My objective for this book—the completely revised and expanded third edition of the *Pen Turner's Workbook*—as well as for all my books is to approach the subject from the mind of the individual asking the question, "How do they do that?" This book will guide you step by step through your journey to creating the fine writing instrument you want to make, whether you want to work with a mother nature inspired piece of wood, an alternative material, or an acrylic blank you cast yourself. This instructional book is the definitive state-of-the-art guide you will need on your quest to learn the skills necessary to make a better pen for yourself and your customer.

This guide will discuss the fundamental skills you need to turn pens as well as the techniques used to create segmented pens and laser cut pens. You'll also learn about working with biologicals, such as antler and snakeskin. All along the way, I'll give you many tips and tricks to make your life easier when creating your masterpieces.

I will assist and guide the individual who has not decided which lathe to purchase and which turning tools are best suited for your particular skill set, and what are some of the other various pieces of shop equipment such as safety equipment and dust collection used in making pens. Tool techniques will be demonstrated to help you build skill quickly and avoid the dreaded dig-in with a skew chisel.

Selecting wood for larger pen styles will be discussed as well as a debate on what is the best pen plating to use in conjunction with any particular pen blank. We will look into wood dyes for coloring your wooden pen blank and alternate ways of preparing the same wooden pen blank to obtain three very distinct outcomes. An expanded "what do I do now" or the "oops" section will show you how to correct some of the common mistakes that everyone makes—myself included.

The book opens with a gallery section with some other very talented pen makers' favorite masterpieces they have created. And the book closes with a gallery section to provide you with some ideas on how to market and display your work to maximize your efforts.

As I have stated in the past, life is too short to carry an ugly pen, so please join me in the workshop, and let's get busy creating that one-of-a-kind fine writing instrument you will be proud to use and display!

You'll learn how to make terrific pens like these by following the instructions in this book.

# PART 1

# Gallery of Pens

There are many very talented and skillful artisans who create wonderful, handmade, one-of-a-kind fine writing instruments. The pens that you will see in this gallery show the work of some of these "master pen makers." The artists include Brian Gisi, Richard Kleinhenz, Anthony Turchetta, Mark Gisi, Seamus Rooney, Glenn McCullough, and myself—all of whom are members of the prestigious Pen Makers Guild. However, the gallery is just a sampling of work. There are many more very talented pen makers who are part of this organization, and everyone in the guild shares their experience and knowledge so that each member's skill level can progress.

As your ability improves with each pen, the challenge will be to seek out other pen makers who could offer a different approach to pen making and to see if that method could be adapted to your individual style. The Internet is a great tool to research and discover other skilled craftsman. Observe them and absorb the information they offer on pen making because that will increase your ability to manufacture one-of-a-kind pens. I hope you enjoy these fine writing instruments!

This amazing array of pens is featured on the gallery pages.

# BARRY GROSS

Elegant Beauty and Tycoon pens feature real snakeskin cast into the acrylic resin.

Tycoon Stars & Stripes, El Presidente green-dyed buckeye burl, closed-end Statesman amboyna burl with cigar label.

These pens feature Gatsby-style pen kits with Kallenshaan Woods laser-cut kits.

These pens are made using my new techniques for casting acrylic resin (see page 115). From left, Captain Morgan spiced rum label pen, watch pieces pen, and clear-cast Sierra Vista fishing fly lures.

These closed-end pens feature clear-cast cigar bands, with a custom cigar box to match the cigar bands.

The top pen is made from a shotgun shell with pheasant feathers and antler. The pen on the right is made from walrus oosik with a Gatsby pen kit.

# RICHARD KLEINHENZ

Richard Kleinhenz is a member of the Pen Maker's Guild and has been creating beautiful pens as a hobby since the mid-1990s. He uses both a wood lathe and a metal lathe to make his pens from a variety of materials.

The top pen is made from a hard, rubber material called Cumberland. The closed-end shape is turned on a pin chuck. The center band and finial trim is also made from Cumberland. The bottom pen is an 18-karat Swiss rose gold regency pen made of katalox.

# SEAMUS ROONEY

Seamus Rooney is a member of the Pen Maker's Guild who uses a scroll saw to cut his coins and casts them in clear resin to create these wonderful pens. Seamus has been casting pens for over six years and has developed his own special style.

Seamus Rooney's Titanic pen (top) is an Emperor Rollerball. He replaced the cap with a liquid-filled compass and layered the barrel with three coins in clear-cast acrylic. Australian pen (middle) is an Atrax fountain pen with a coin pierced and clear casted. At bottom, the pen barrel is a 30-06 Upshaw bullet with a pierced Texas quarter and clear cast in polyresin.

SCOTT KRINER

# GLENN MCCULLOUGH

Glenn McCullough is an independent pen maker who incorporates exotic woods, antler, and resins into his pens. The accents he uses are precious metals such as rhodium, platinum, titanium, and sterling silver. Glenn is a member of the Pen Maker's Guild.

McCullough's Junior Retro rhodium rollerball is made from Trustone, Corian, acrylic, and guitar pick guard material.

Glenn McCullough presents a gentleman's rhodium fountain pen in curly koa and alternative casein.

McCullough's Platinum El Presidente curly ash and black acrylic pen incorporates guitar pick guard material and sterling silver wire accents.

# ANTHONY TURCHETTA

Anthony Turchetta has been making pens for over ten years and creates a number of fascinating pieces using many acrylic type materials. Anthony is also a member of the Pen Makers Guild as well as other pen making groups.

*Amber Ripple*, a closed-end fountain pen, is made from Italian Lucite with a 14-karat solid gold nib.

This statesman fountain pen is made from orange and black swirl ebonite with a 14-karat solid gold nib. The rope pattern was cut on a legacy mill and then hand sanded.

# BRIAN AND MARK GISI

Brian and Mark Gisi are a father-and-son team who are both members of the Pen Makers Guild. They started with a pen turning class at a local woodworking store over ten years ago and they have advanced pen making to another level. Brian calls this latest series his "exoskeleton" series and Mark still uses very complicated segmented pieces to create is works of art.

Carbon Torpedo pen by Brian Gisi features integrated hand-carved aluminum support structures with titanium rod accents. Brian has incorporated carbon fiber tubes and support beams with an intricate fin system of plate titanium.

Brian Gisi's Black Widow pen features hand-cut titanium plates fitted over a carbon fiber tube with hand-turned acrylic and aluminum frame components assembled with more than 50 brass screws.

Mark Gisi combines rosewood cylinders and titanium bars with amboyna and buckeye burls in random angle patterns, accented with orange and black Gisi Designs with a custom carbon fiber clip.

Mark Gisi accents green-dyed buckeye and acrylics with color grain in vee and straight line patterns. The fine lines are made from green and white Gisi Designs accenting material with a custom carbon fiber clip.

SCOTT KRINER

# PART 2

# Pen Turning Basics

Creating and turning pens is an exciting hobby that will afford you hours of enjoyment and relaxation. The thrill of creating something useful and beautiful with your own hands from the variety of materials available to pen turners, will keep you engaged for quite a long time. Stunning pens can be turned using everything from manmade materials to wood and acrylics you cast yourself. This section will show you the particulars of mini-lathes and turning tools, materials for pens, and basic turning techniques from the perspective and the goal of turning great pens.

**The skew chisel** cuts a smooth and clean surface on the pen blank.

# CHAPTER 1

# Setting Up Shop

The heart of your workshop will be your lathe. If you have yet to purchase one or if you are looking to purchase a new one, I have included some guidelines to aid you in your decision-making process. We'll also take a look at some of the other tools that are useful when making pens.

## Choosing a lathe

Purchasing a lathe is a personal choice, and one that cannot be made solely on the recommendations of others! When considering the purchase of a lathe, take time to ask yourself the following questions.

### What Type of Turning Will You Want to Accomplish?

Lathes come in a variety of sizes and styles, and it is important to identify the type of turning you would like to do before you make a purchase. Investing in the wrong type of lathe can limit the number and variety of pieces that you can create. And, if you are a beginner, the wrong type of lathe purchase can make your first turning experience less than wonderful!

For this book, I used a variable-speed mini-lathe. As the name suggests, mini-lathes are smaller than regular full-size lathes (see **Figure 1.2**) and are particularly well suited to smaller projects such as pens, pencils, bottle stoppers, ornaments, boxes, smaller bowls, and vessels (see **Figure 1.1**).

**Figure 1.1.** Mini-lathes, like this Jet mini-lathe, are smaller than regular-size lathes and are well suited to smaller projects.

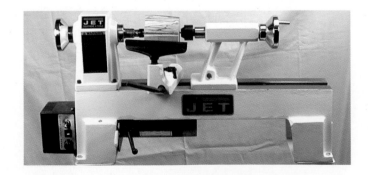

### Will You Concentrate your Energies Strictly on Pens?

Turning is a great hobby and, even if you only turn pens, there will be more than enough pens to keep you very busy. Pens come in all shapes and sizes and can be made from a variety of materials including, but not limited to, all sorts of domestic and exotic hardwoods, stabilized woods, antler, plastics, acrylics, and solid surface materials such as Corian.

In this book, you will learn how to turn many different pen styles. You will also learn to turn a sampling of some of the most common materials used in turning pens. Using your imagination to combine different styles and materials will keep you busy with a never- ending array of projects for your new hobby.

### Are You Interested in Turning Smaller Bowls or Vessels Now or Possibly in the Future?

As mentioned before, the mini-lathe is a great tool for a variety of additional small projects, including miniature bowls, lidded boxes, assorted spindle projects, and much more. If you are even remotely interested in expanding your hobby to include more than pens, you'll want to take that interest into consideration when choosing a lathe.

## How Much Money Are You Willing to Commit to your Purchase?

Lathes vary greatly in price depending on the manufacturer and the accessories included. General pricing can run anywhere from around one hundred to hundreds of dollars. Again, think long and hard about how you want to use your lathe. Buying a more expensive lathe now may make better use of your money than buying an inexpensive lathe and then a second more expensive lathe shortly thereafter.

## How Much Room Do You Have to Devote to your Lathe?

Mini-lathes are just that: miniature lathes. They measure approximately three feet across and about one foot wide. They are perfectly suited to smaller workshop areas, such as those in a garage or a corner of a basement. My mini-lathe fits comfortably in my one-car garage, and it shares that space with a dust collector, a band saw, a contractor's table saw, a scroll saw, a wide variety of shop tools, and uncounted blocks and boards of wood that will soon turn into beautiful lathe projects.

## Are You Interested in a Floor-Mounted Lathe or a Benchtop Lathe?

Your choice of a floor-mounted lathe or a benchtop lathe is determined by the amount of workspace you have (see **Figures 1.1 and 1.2**). Choose a benchtop lathe if space is limited. If you choose a benchtop lathe, make sure that the bench is positioned correctly so that you aren't turning on a lathe that's too low or too high. Make sure that your lathe is bolted to your bench top to avoid vibration. A floor-mounted lathe should have a sturdy mount, preferably one specifically designed for the lathe.

**Figure 1.2**. A floor-mounted lathe, like this 14" Jet lathe, will work well for a variety of projects if you have the necessary space for it in your workshop.

## Do You Want a Belt-Driven Lathe or One with a Variable Speed Control?

Switching belts can take time out of your schedule, and, if you are someone who has a limited amount of time to turn, you may opt for the variable speed control (see **Figure 1.3**). Since the first edition of *The Pen Turner's Workbook* was written, I have switched over to a variable-speed mini-lathe for both the convenience of not having to change belts and the ease of use when applying my finishes.

**Figure 1.3**. A lathe that requires switching belts to change speeds can be very inefficient if time is limited. Lathes with variable-speed controls (inset) change speeds with the simple turn of a knob.

# TIPS FOR CHOOSING A MINI-LATHE

1. Visit various woodworking outlets and inspect the lathes for the features that are important to you.

2. Check the Internet for reviews of the lathe you are interested in purchasing.

3. Personally test as many of these lathes as you can. Do not just let the salesperson demonstrate the lathe to you. In most cases, the salesperson will be very proficient on his or her piece of equipment.

4. Turn the lathe on and listen to it. Change speeds on the lathe either by changing the belt (now you will see how difficult it is to change the speed) or by using the dial on the lathe with a variable speed control.

5. Place your hand on the headstock and note how much vibration the lathe is generating. Conduct the point-to-point test (**see Figure 1.4**). Insert a drive spur with a point into the headstock and insert a live center with a point into the tailstock and bring the two together. Now turn the lathe on and check for accuracy. If the points do not line up precisely point to point even while running, walk away and do not look back, even if the salesperson is offering a "great" deal. If the lathe doesn't run straight, nothing you turn will be straight. Remember the old axiom: it is always best to afford the best you can because quality usually is reflective of the price.

6. Finally, check that the lathe you intend to purchase is manufactured by a reputable company, and find out exactly what the warranty includes.

**Figure 1.4**. Check the accuracy of the lathe by doing a point-to-point test with the headstock and the tailstock.

# Ancillary equipment

There is always something new in the pen-making world. The following pieces of equipment and accessories are not necessary, but they are nice to have because they offer you faster and easier ways to prepare your pen blanks.

**Drill press and drill-centering vise:** These are used to center and drill perfectly vertical holes in your pen blanks in preparation for inserting the brass pen tubes (see **Figure 1.5**).

**Barrel trimmer and hand drill:** These tools are used to square the end of the pen blank to the barrel of the pen tube (see **Figure 1.6**). As an alternative, make a squaring jig for the disk sander (**Figure 1.11**).

**Band saw, chop saw, or table saw:** A chop saw or table saw can reduce boards to pen blank material. A band saw also can reduce large burls or irregular stock (see **Figure 1.7**).

**Grinding system:** To sharpen your tools, you will need to have a grinding system. A bench grinder is an ideal way to sharpen your turning tools. For beginners, and even for turners with experience, grinding jigs offer the best solution for placing sharp, consistent edges on your tools (see **Figure 1.8**).

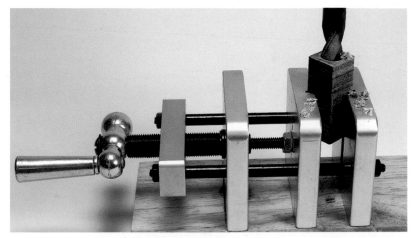

**Figure 1.5.** A drill-centering vise helps you precisely drill a vertical hole through the pen blank.

**Figure 1.6.** A barrel trimmer squares the end of the pen blank with the inside of the pen tube.

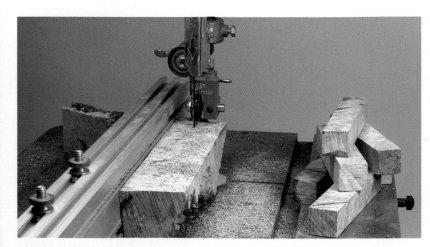

**Figure 1.7.** Use a band saw or a table saw to cut your own pen blanks to size.

**Figure 1.8.** A bench grinder puts a sharp edge on your turning tools.

**Figure 1.9.** A drilling chuck mounted in the headstock can hold the blank for drilling centered holes.

**Figure 1.10.** Lubricate drill bits to reduce burning from friction.

**Drilling chuck:** If you do not have a drill press or even if you do, this lathe accessory will prove invaluable in drilling straight holes in your pen blanks (see **Figure 1.9**).

**Drill lube:** Spray Dri-Cote lubricant on your drill bits prior to drilling to reduce frictional burning (**Figure 1.10**).

**Squaring jig and disc sander:** Instead of using a barrel trimmer to square the ends of the pen blank, a squaring jig and disc sander can be used (**Figure 1.11**).

**Acrylic pen buffing system:** Use this buffing setup to remove any scratches from acrylic material. Once you buff your pens you will never go back to not buffing them! This accessory will also aid in finishing antler and all CA finishes (**Figure 1.12**).

**Figure 1.11.** A disk-sander squaring jig, made from aluminum angle iron, puts a square end on a pen blank.

**Figure 1.12.** Soft cloth buffing wheels charged with polishing compound will put a gleam on most finishes.

# Selecting pen turning tools

There are many manufacturers of turning tools today. Search the Internet for turning tools and you will be inundated with information on turning tools and the numerous companies that make them. You will find that each company claims its tools are the best and will give you the cleanest cut while holding an edge longer than any of its competitors. The reality of the situation for today's turning needs is that you have two main choices: You can choose carbon steel tools or you can choose tools made of high-speed steel (HSS).

Carbon steel tools are just that: tools made from carbon steel. These tools are not as expensive as tools made from high-speed steel. Carbon steel tools will not keep a sharp edge as long as high-speed steel and will dull faster depending on the material you will be cutting.

There are many grades of high-speed steel. They are identified by M1, M2, M7, and M50, with M1 being the most expensive grade and also the most brittle. Today, most of the high-speed steel tools are made from the M2-grade high-speed steel or better. When turning woods and plastics, all grades of high-speed steel tools will far outlast the lesser expensive carbon steel tools. For my money, the high-speed steel is a better value. Because everyone has his own budget, only you can decide which will be the better value for your own dollar.

Now that you have selected which steel you want, which manufacturer do you purchase from? There are many reputable manufacturers of turning tools. Here again, the Internet can be a valuable resource in choosing the correct manufacturer for your needs.

The basic turning tools that I recommend to my students are sometimes packaged as a set or can be purchased separately. The high-speed steel set of pen-making tools (see **Figure 1.13**) consists of a ⅛" parting tool, a ⁵⁄₁₆" roughing gouge, a ¼" spindle gouge (see **Figure 1.14**), a ½" skew (see **Figure 1.15**), and a ½" Spindlemaster (a unique tool that is a cross between a skew and a spindle gouge). (The skew has received a lot of bad press, and it has been labeled the "white knuckle" tool because it is a difficult tool to master when you are just beginning your turning experience. However, with a little practice it is a very valuable tool with many purposes, including extra-clean finishing cuts.) This basic set of turning tools will offer the broadest range for both pen turning and smaller projects.

**Figure 1.13.** Pictured from top to bottom: a ⅛" parting tool, a ⁵⁄₁₆" roughing gouge, a ¼" spindle gouge, a ½" skew, and a ½" Spindlemaster (a unique tool that is a cross between a skew and a spindle gouge).

**Figure 1.14.** A spindle gouge is used primarily for turning beads and coves on pens. It is a good addition to a beginner's toolbox.

**Figure 1.15.** A skew is a difficult tool to master, but, once you have learned how to use it, it will become a heavy hitter in your arsenal of turning tools.

### Turning Tools for the 'Sharpening Challenged'

A dull tool can be dangerous and will not offer the best finish for your work in progress. If you are having difficulty sharpening your tools or you cannot keep a sharp edge on them, there are turning tools on the market that have replaceable carbide tips that are coated with titanium nitride (see **Figure 1.16**). The titanium nitride coating offers a longer tip life at higher turning speeds and aids in producing smoother surfaces for your project while maintaining a longer-lasting, sharper cutting edge.

**Figure 1.16.** Tools with replaceable carbide tips provide an alternative to sharpening.

Using the nitride-coated tip technology offers the turner with no sharpening skills the ability to change a dull edge to a sharp edge with little effort.

### Mandrels

You will need to purchase a mandrel if you want to make pens. A mandrel is a round steel rod that is held in the lathe headstock spindle (see **Figure 1.17**). The headstock will have a morse taper hole in the spindle that will either be a #1 morse taper or a #2 morse taper. For example, the Jet mini-lathe, the Delta midi-lathe, and the Fisch lathe all use a #2 morse taper, whereas the Carba-Tec and Sherline lathes use #1 morse tapers. Check the lathe you purchase to obtain the mandrel with the correct morse taper.

Mandrels come in two sizes, 7mm or 8mm, with either adjustable or fixed lengths. On some 7mm mandrels, the center rod can be adjustable. The advantage to the adjustable mandrel is that the shaft can be moved in or out to any length to suit a number of different pen blanks without using spacer bushings. Also, if you choose to turn just one piece of the pen at a time, this is your best choice for a mandrel. The 8mm mandrel is sometimes called a precision mandrel, which incorporates a thicker-diameter center steel rod than the standard 7mm mandrel. This thicker-diameter center steel rod helps to prevent "whip" while turning. Whip occurs when extensive pressure is placed on the tailstock, causing the end of the mandrel to whip, or not to turn evenly. This motion will cause your pen blank to turn oval instead of round. Some pen kit manufacturers like this thicker mandrel for their larger-style pens. Another accessory to help minimize whip is a mandrel saver tailstock center (**Figure 1.18**). This product will slide directly over the 7mm (A) mandrel and press against

**7mm (A)**

**8mm (B)**

**Figure 1.17.** A good mandrel is a necessity for pen turning. A 7mm mandrel, sometimes called an A mandrel, is shown on top, and an 8mm mandrel, sometimes called a B mandrel, is shown on the bottom.

the bushings with no pressure on the mandrel shaft, thus helping you make a more concentric turning. When you purchase a pen kit, the manufacturer of the kit will inform you which mandrel it uses.

## Turning Between Centers

Turning between centers (TBC) does not use a mandrel and will necessitate a few additional tools (**Figure 1.19**). The popularity of TBC is on the rise, because with this system you will get a more concentric and therefore better turning. By not using mandrels you will greatly reduce if not eliminate the whip action associated with standard mandrels. To get started turning between centers you will need the following items: a 60° dead center to be mounted into the headstock of the lathe and a 60° live center to be mounted into the tailstock of your lathe (**Figure 1.20**). Before you buy these accessories, you need to know if your headstock and tailstock have a #1 Morse taper or a #2 MT. Just because you have a 60° dead and live center does not automatically mean you will get a better turning if your lathe is not in proper alignment. Mount both centers and make sure they match up point to point (**Figure 1.21**).

You'll also need a different set of bushings that are designed for turning between centers. They can be made from steel or from Delrin plastic (see **Figure 1.22**). The TBC bushings have a deeper chamfer than regular bushings and they are longer, so they penetrate deep into the pen tube and give it more stability. Steel bushings will last a lot longer than Delrin, but Delrin bushings have one distinct advantage over steel—they do not leave behind gray steel dust that could contaminate lighter colored woods when sanding.

**Figure 1.18.** The mandrel saver (left) fits right over the regular tailstock live center.

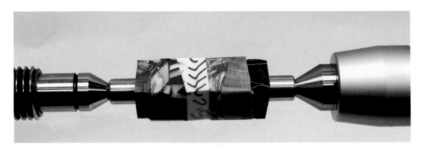

**Figure 1.19.** Turning between centers does not use a mandrel but does require a 60° dead center in the headstock (left), and a 60° live center in the tailstock (right).

**Figure 1.20.** The 60° centers fit into the lathe spindles with #1 or #2 Morse tapers.

**Figure 1.21.** For accurate turning the lathe centers must meet precisely point to point.

**Figure 1.22.** Bushings made of steel (left) or Delrin plastic (right) mount the blank between the 60° centers

## Safety in the workshop

We all know which practices are safe and which ones can be dangerous when working in the shop. However, the reality is that we do not always practice what we know to be the right thing to do! When it comes to using a lathe, it is important to do the right thing or you can get into trouble very fast. By observing the following few safety tips, we can have a safer work environment to spur the creative genius inside us all.

**Figure 1.23.** Keep loose hair and clothing away from the lathe.

**Figure 1.24.** A dust collection system will remove dust and chips from the air as you turn. Coupled with a dust mask, this system will provide solid protection for your respiratory system.

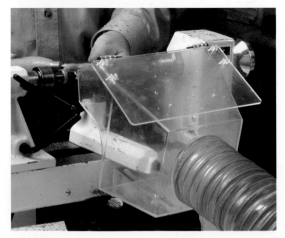

*Wear protective eyeglasses and/or a full face shield.* This is the most obvious safety tip, and, believe it or not, it is also the one that is most ignored. It only takes one small flying chip to scratch your cornea; and then in the back of your mind you can hear your mother say, "See, I told you it would take your eye out!" The moral is wear eye protection!

*Do not wear loose clothing or jewelry or have long hair dangling around your work in progress.* Pull back your hair by putting it in a ponytail or under a hat, and remove any loose jewelry (see **Figure 1.23**). Tuck in shirttails and roll up sleeves or leave them buttoned. Do not lean over the lathe while it is running because it may just catch your clothing!

Do not touch your work piece while it is in motion on the lathe. This sounds simple, but people still have a tendency to touch a work piece while it is still moving. If you must touch it, do so lightly and on the top of the work. Never touch the work piece in front of the tool rest where your finger can get caught in between the tool rest and the work piece. That will definitely make you a very unhappy person!

*Dust collection of some form is a must!* When used in conjunction with the dust collection hood attached to the back of the lathe (see **Figure 1.24**), the one-horsepower dust collector located to the left of the lathe will remove most of the airborne dust particles as you are turning and sanding (see **Figure 1.25**). It offers strong suction to draw dust away from the operator.

A stand-alone dust mask used in conjunction with this system will offer solid dust protection to the operator. However, if this type of collection system is not available, a dust mask of some type would be a minimum for respiratory protection. This measure is necessary because some woods can be toxic to individuals who are sensitive to particular woods, such as rosewood, cocobolo, and many spalted woods.

The best protection offered is a combination face shield with air filtration. This type of lightweight system combines a face and eye shield with respiratory protection, which is a great addition to any shop (see **Figure 1.26**).

***Be relaxed in front of your lathe.*** A good starting position when standing in front of your lathe should be with your feet about shoulders' width apart (see **Figure 1.27**). The centerline of your pen should be slightly above or in line with your elbow when your elbow is in a resting position by your side.

***Proper lighting is a must.*** You have to see your work before you can effectively turn your work (see **Figure 1.28**).

**Figure 1.25.** A dust collector will remove most airborne dust particles created by turning and sanding.

**Figure 1.26.** Protection from dust is essential. Use a dust ventilation system, as shown here, or any combination of other dust collection/protection devices on the market.

**Figure 1.27.** A comfortable stance is important when you are working at your mini-lathe. Stand with your feet about shoulders' width apart. Your elbow should be even with or slightly above the level of the piece you are turning.

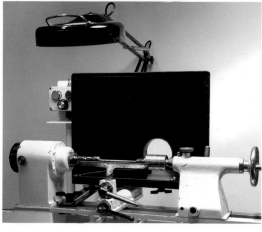

**Figure 1.28.** Shop set-up includes not just a good lathe, but good lighting and dust protection as well.

# CHAPTER 2

# Selecting Materials

There are a number of materials that will make a beautiful pen—from common wood to snakeskin. Because wood is so popular, we'll discuss several aspects of wood as they relate to pen turning. We'll also look at some of the characteristics of non-wood materials.

## Wood

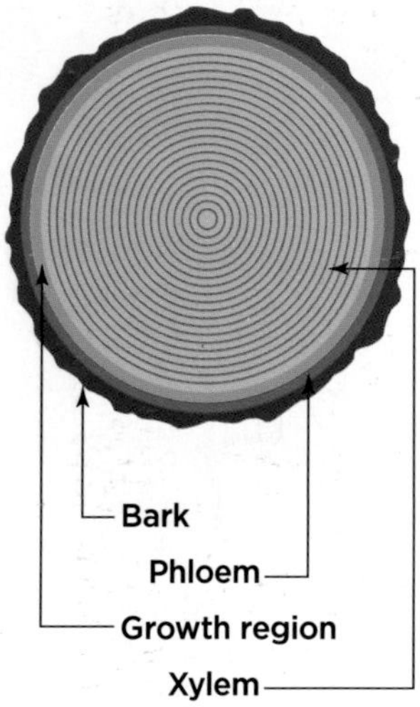

Bark
Phloem
Growth region
Xylem

**Figure 2.1.** This illustration shows the interior of a living tree.

Trees, a penmaker's friend . . . According to the Greek legend, the Greek god Adonis was said to have been born of a tree. He gave to humanity the strength of the woody core, the upward-reaching soul of the sky-seeking branches, and a root system deep within Mother Earth that ties our hearts to the center of the world.

Trees are the longest-living and largest living organisms on Earth. Currently the world's tallest tree is a coast redwood tree from California, standing over 360 feet tall. The bristlecone pines located in the United States are confirmed to be the world's oldest trees with ages up to 4,600 years.

Numerous sources have stated that the actual number of tree species may well exceed 50,000. Since the beginning of time, trees have played a significant part in the survival of mankind. In 50 years, one tree can recycle more than $37,000 worth of water, provide $31,000 worth of erosion control, and offer $62,000 worth of air pollution control. Why, just two mature trees provide enough oxygen for a family of four and assist in reducing the greenhouse effect by absorbing carbon dioxide. Trees are excellent noise barriers, quieting highway noise for nearby neighborhoods. They also provide a soothing effect for patients in hospitals who have a view of trees. Finally, trees provide us

with food, shelter, and, for the purpose of this book, excellent material for wooden pens!

### Anatomy of a Tree

Let us dissect the basic anatomy of a tree without becoming botanists (see **Figure 2.1**). The outer bark is a corky material that protects the main trunk of the tree. Directly beneath the outer bark is a layer of inner bark called phloem. The phloem is made of tubes that transport food and sugars throughout the tree. Inside the phloem is the cambium layer of the tree, which usually feels slimy in a freshly cut trunk. The cambium layer produces phloem (bark tissue) and xylem (wood tissue). The living xylem cells, called sapwood, carry water and minerals from the roots to the leaves. The sapwood lies in a broad ring around the darker heartwood and often is whitish or cream colored. As the sapwood cells die, they fill with organic material and become the heartwood of the tree, which is the darker inner portion of the tree. **Figures 2.2 and 2.3** depict a piece of cocobolo with heartwood and sapwood and then two pens made from this piece of wood. The top pen was made without the sapwood, while the bottom one shows both heartwood and sapwood.

## Learning to Think Small

Now that we know enough about a tree's anatomy to be dangerous, which portion of the tree makes the best-looking pen blank for a woodturner's needs? Sapwood or heartwood or combinations of both make impressive pens. Burls, which are abnormal growths on trees, make stunning pens. Straight grain, cross grain, or end grain adds more possibilities. When it comes to choosing a wood, "so many choices, so little time" is a phrase that comes to mind. Let's take a closer look at some of those choices.

There are many choices of woods and grain patterns. One problem we have as penmakers is that oftentimes we do not think small. A very beautiful piece of quilted maple with a lot of character may look beautiful as a large table. However, when it is reduced to the size of a pen blank, you probably will not get any of the quilting, and thus your pen blank will appear very boring.

When thinking of any wood that you like, you must be able to picture that particular material in a ¾" x ¾" x 5" pen blank. If you are not sure if a piece of wood will look good as a pen, put it to the "look small" test (see **Figures 2.4** and **2.5**). Take a piece of clear acrylic ⅛" x ¾" x 5" and lay it over the piece of wood you are considering using as a pen blank. If the piece you choose has a lot of character or you see a lot of grain underneath the acrylic, then it probably will make a great-looking pen. Remember to think small!

**Figures 2.2 and 2.3.** The lower photo is a slab of cocobolo wood that includes both heartwood and sapwood. The upper photo shows two pens that were made from this piece of cocobolo wood. The top pen was made without the sapwood, while the bottom one is part heartwood and part sapwood.

**Figure 2.4.** The grain in this piece of fishtail oak will create an interesting pen.

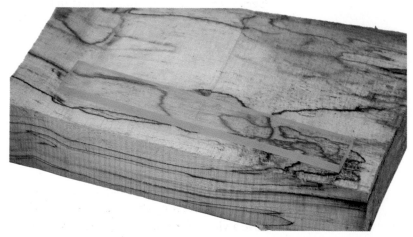

**Figure 2.5.** The dark lines in this spalted maple will make a unique pen.

**Figure 2.6.** Pen blanks comes in several standard sizes: ½", ⅝", ¾", and ⅞".

**Figure 2.7.** The outgrowths on trees are called burls. They are actually tree limbs that did not grow correctly.

## Pen Blank Size

Pen blank sizes vary depending on the pen style you choose, from the very smallest ½" x ½" x 5" for a slimline pen style (this leaves no room for error) to the jumbo blanks measuring ⅞" x ⅞" x 5" for the larger pens such as the Statesman, Majestic, or El Grande (see **Figure 2.6**).

## Burls

The most desirable of all material, in this author's opinion, is the burl. A burl is a hard, woody, often flattened, hemispherical outgrowth on a tree: basically, a benign tree tumor (see **Figure 2.7**). Burls start to form when twig bud cells fail to grow normally to form limbs. Instead, the bud cells just continue to multiply and multiply, growing in a round growth with an irregular grain pattern. This is not good for the tree because it did not grow a normal limb, but it's great for us turners!

We all have seen them but probably have just overlooked them not knowing what they were. After all, these limb burls can grow with no detrimental effect to the tree. Think of them as benign tumors for a tree. **Figure 2.8** is a photograph of an oak burl. **Figure 2.9** is a close-up of a maple burl. Note the swirl pattern and raised bumps or "eyes." Burls make very pleasing pens because of the irregular grain pattern (see **Figure 2.10**).

**Figure 2.8.** All trees are susceptible to burls. This is a photo of a burl from an oak tree.

**Figure 2.9.** Because of the way burls grow, they often have very interesting grains. Note the swirl pattern and the raised bumps, or "eyes," in this close-up shot of a maple burl.

**Figure 2.10.** The unusual grain pattern of burls lends itself to stunning pens. In the author's opinion, there is no better wood for pen turning.

## Cutting on Angles

The three pens shown in **Figure 2.11** were all made from the same piece of zebrawood. Just because you use the same wood for a dozen pens does not mean they all have to look identical. One way to get more variety from your wood supply is to cut the pen blanks on different angles. Cutting on a different angle will cause the grain to run in a different direction, which will offer you a greater variability in your finished pen product.

Take another look at the three pens in Figure 2.11. The three pens were all made from the same piece of zebrawood. However, all three pen blanks were prepared differently. The pen blank on the left was cut cross grain, the middle blank was cut on a 15-degree angle, and the blank on the right was cut parallel to the grain. While it's obvious that all three pens were made from zebrawood, the look of each pen is unique.

Another example of a wood that looks very different when cut on an angle is cocobolo. Cutting the pen blank on a slight angle of approximately 15 degrees opens up the grain, giving it a dramatic effect and thus creating a more appealing pen for someone to purchase.

Look at the bird's-eye maple example in **Figure 2.12**. The pen blank on the bottom is running parallel to the grain, and the blank that is directly above it will be cut on an angle to open up the grain and offer more enhancement of the pen.

The box elder slab in **Figure 2.13** is showing a blank that will be cut on an angle. When the pen is made, the grain will appear more open, or more visible, because it was prepared on an angle.

**Figure 2.11.** By cutting the blocks of wood at three different angles, you can get three very different-looking pens. These three pens were all cut from the same piece of zebrawood.

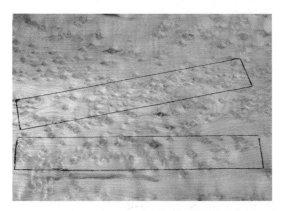

**Figure 2.12.** This piece of bird's-eye maple will be cut two ways—once along the grain and once at a 15-degree angle—to create two unique pens.

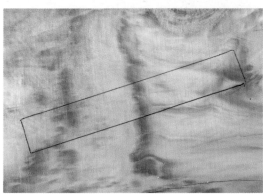

**Figure 2.13.** This box elder blank will be cut on an angle. The red coloring running through the block is actually the result of a disease.

**Figure 2.14.** These rhodium-coated slimline pens were turned from thuya burl.

**Figure 2.15.** This El Presidente fountain pen displays beautiful amboyna burl.

**Figure 2.16.** Snakeskin coated with acrylic was the medium for this statesman junior rollerball pen.

## Exotic Hardwood

With over 50,000 different species of wood to choose from, it would take you over 137 years to make one pen per day from all 50,000 trees. So, which woods make the best pens? That is a question of personal taste.

It's important to remember that just because you like a certain wood does not mean that the general public will agree. Experience will tell you what sells and what makes a good-looking pen. It has been my experience that any tight-grained burls always sell well and make a smart-looking pen. Thuya burl, amboyna burl, and snakewood are just a few of my personal favorites, which have sold very well at pen shows (see **Figures 2.14**, **2.15**, and **2.16**).

If you do work with exotic woods, remember that dust from exotic woods, such as cocobolo and rosewood, has been shown to cause sensitivity from the wood dust and is possibly carcinogenic, meaning that dust masks coupled with dust collection systems are imperative. You'll also want to be sure that you buy exotic woods from reputable dealers.

## Stabilized Wood

There has been a massive resurgence in the stabilized wood market. Wood that is normally difficult to turn because it is soft and crumbling, such as spalted material, can now be turned into masterpieces that retain all of the wood's natural beauty thanks to the stabilization process (see **Figure 2.17**).

Stabilization uses high pressure to force liquid acrylic resins into wood fibers. The resins completely impregnate the wood and then cure it. Once stabilized, the wood increases in weight by 20 to 150 percent (porous woods, such as spalted material, take on more resin than dense woods such as cocobolo or ebony). The stabilized pen blank becomes harder and stronger, and the color of the wood (if it is a lighter wood) may darken slightly.

Because the acrylic saturated the wood fibers, you can turn cross grain without the fear of end grain tearout! When cutting end grain, the cutting tool is forced across the wood fibers, causing them to tear. Since stabilized wood is impregnated with resin, you will not have any grain to worry about. An additional plus to the stabilization process is that dyes can be added to the wood to penetrate deep into the fibers of the wood while it is being processed, thus producing dramatic results (see **Figures 2.18** and **2.19**).

**Figure 2.17.** This Statesman fountain pen is made of stabilized spalted mango.

**Figure 2.18.** Stabilized and dyed pen blanks are available in a wide variety of colors.

**Figure 2.19.** Double dyed buckeye burl. Double dyeing is taking two contrasting colors and injecting them into the wood to accentuate the natural grain.

**Figure 2.20.** Cream colored Alumilite casting resin has been mixed with coffee beans (bottom), rotini pasta (middle), and split peas (top) to create these interesting pen blanks.

## Alternative materials

With each new edition of the *Pen Turner's Workbook*, more and more new materials for pen turners keep surfacing. From coffee beans, split peas, and pasta to acorns, snakeskins, and feathers, if a material can hold a pen tube, then someone will be creative enough to make it into a pen blank. Another option, which is becoming more popular, is casting your own blanks using a variety of materials; this technique will be discussed in detail on page 115.

**Figure 2.21.** Real snakeskin has been wrapped around a pen tube and coated with clear acrylic to create this imaginative set.

**Figure 2.22.** Acrywood pen blanks are made using the caps sawn from burls mixed with different colored Alumilite casting resin.

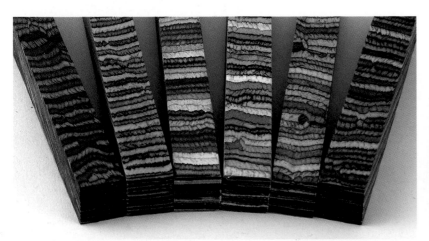

**Figure 2.23.** Color Grain is made from resin-impregnated dye and laminated colored hardwood veneer.

**Figure 2.24.** Corian is a solid surface substance that is commonly used for kitchen and vanity countertops. It is easy to turn and creates an interesting pen that feels good in the writer's hand.

**Figure 2.25.** Inlace is a unique acrylic compound that comes in a variety of colors. Pens turned from blocks of Inlace are popular among pen buyers because of their interesting color combinations.

**Figure 2.26.** Predrilled 7mm Aquapearl pen blanks are made from an acrylic material that emulates the contrasting shades of real pearl.

**Figure 2.27.** Crushed velvet pen blanks are made from another acrylic material that offers fewer colors.

**Figure 2.28.** Yet another interesting material is Polygem. This acrylic compound mimics the colors of stones, minerals, and gems that appear in nature.

**Figure 2.29.** Mica Swirl pen blanks are made from polyester and resin. As the pen blanks are hardening, the swirls are mixed to form patterns.

**Figure 2.30.** Antler and buffalo horn are easy to turn with sharp tools; however, the odor when drilling the blanks can be unpleasant.

**Figure 2.31.** Colored Alumilite casting resin was mixed with acorns to create these visually pleasing pen blanks.

**Figure 2.32.** These Genesis pen blanks are an Inlace Acrylester variant, which offers enhanced color effects and a truly unique look.

**Figure 2.33.** Acrylic ripple pen blanks are offered in a large variety of colors boasting a striking line of flowing shapes and threads.

**Figure 2.34.** Trustone pen blanks are made from 85% stone mixed with acrylic plastic. These pen blanks look like genuine stone but they will drill and turn like any other acrylic.

**Figure 2.35.** Pheasant feathers were carefully placed onto pen tubes and then covered with Alumilite casting resin to fashion these stunning pen blanks.

**Figure 2.36.** Exotic animal pen blanks show vibrant colors with zebra, snow leopard, and leopard stripes.

**Figure 2.37.** M3 (Macro Molecular Metal) metal pen blanks are made from 95% source metal combined with chemical binders and acrylic resin. This new material turns and polishes similarly to other acrylic materials.

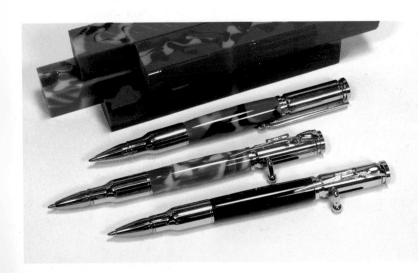

**Figure 2.38.** Camouflage acrylic pen blanks are made for the hunter or someone who just wants to hide the pen they made.

# CHAPTER 3

# Pen Plating and Styles

Once you have selected the material—be it wood, stabilized wood, acrylic, antler, or Corian—you must then choose which pen style you want to create and what plating you want to use. The pen style refers to the overall shape of the pen, whether it is a thin pen, such as a slimline, or a thicker pen, such as a cigar pen. You'll also want to decide if you want to make a ballpoint, a rollerball, or a fountain pen. This will further narrow down your choices. Then, you'll need to decide what plating to use. The plating consists of the outer metal pieces of the pen. The metal cap, clip, center band, and other pieces can be manufactured in a variety of platings. In this section, we'll take a look at the more popular pen and plating styles. To date, there are well over 60 different styles of pens that one can choose to make. No one particular style of pen will suit everyone; that is why there are so many different sizes and styles.

**Figure 3.1.** Smaller pen tubes work for smaller pens; larger pen tubes for larger pens.

**Figure 3.2.** The larger the pen tube, the larger the pen. This Statesman pen kit requires an oversized pen blank.

## Pen styles

One question that students always ask is, "How do you know what shape to make the pen?" My answer is, "Any shape you want!" These are your creations, so why not have the shapes that you want? Just because I, as the author, make a pen a certain way does not mean that every pen on this earth should be made the same way.

Some pen makers turn beads into their pens, other turn captured rings into them. The shape and design of a pen is up to the imagination of the pen maker. I personally do not like absolutely straight pens. Each pen I make has a slight flair to the shape. My first pens were very bulbous in shape, but, after making many pens, I modified the shape slightly to suit what I liked and ultimately what the customer liked.

One limiting factor to the shape of the pen can be the size of the pen tube. Obviously, taking the 7mm pen tubes from a Slimline Pen kit and trying to make a cigar pen out of that kit will not work. (See **Figure 3.1.**) You will never be able to make a slimline 7mm pen tube into a 10mm cigar pen. However, you can make different variations using a Slimline kit (see Project 2, Wire-Burned-

Band Slimline Pen, page 62, and Project 3, Corian Center-Banded Slimline Pen page 64).

It seems obvious, but larger pen tubes make larger pens. For example, the Statesman Pen kit (see **Figure 3.2**) tubes will fit inside an oversized pen blank ⅞" x ⅞" x 5" that is drilled with two different drill bits of ¹⁵⁄₃₂" and ³⁷⁄₆₄" in size. Note the difference in just the pen tubes of the Slimline and the Statesman Pen kits (see **Figure 3.3**).

If you are still unsure how to shape the overall pen, look where you purchased the pen kit or check a catalog to see what shape is recommended for that particular style of pen. Remember, each pen is a reflection of your work and personality: Make it good!

When you make a pen, the kit instructions will generally have a picture or an illustration of the suggested shape, but that is only a suggestion. The decision is yours, not the pen kit manufacturer's.

In conversations with several of the leading pen kit manufacturers, the golden rule of ⁸⁄₁₀ is still very much in effect. Of the active pen makers, 20 percent of them make 80 percent of all the pens. Given all the different varieties of pen kits and plating options, the most popular pen kit is still the Slimline kit. While other pens are popular, the Slimline is still the one kit that is purchased the most from the manufacturers.

In my opinion, the slimline's popularity is due to the fact that most instructors teach beginning pen turning using a slimline pen because it is the easiest and fastest to make. After leaving a class, students want to be able to repeat what they just made, so they buy more Slimline Pen kits to practice and learn.

The Slimline kit is versatile because many different shapes can be made with this pen kit. In **Figure 3.4**, the pen on top does not use the metal center band and was turned thicker in the center to give it the appearance

of a pen different from a slimline. The middle pen is slightly thicker than the pen on the bottom, but all three pens were made from a Slimline Pen kit. Use your imagination and be creative by changing the shape of the pen to make your own unique pen style!

On the page that follows, you will find a chart listing some of the more popular styles of pens and the platings that are offered by each pen. This is by no means a complete listing of all of the pens or all of the platings, but it is a good place to start your search for the perfect pen!

**Figure 3.3.** Note the difference between the tube sizes for a slimline pen (inside) and the tubes for a Statesman pen (outside).

**Figure 3.4.** Not all pens from one kit need to be the same shape. Note the different shapes from this Slimline kit.

| PEN STYLE NAME | 24kt plating | Upgrade Gold Plating | Gold Titanium Nitride | Black Titanium Nitride | Brushed Satin | Black Enamel | Gun Metal | Chrome | Rhodium/ Platinum | Sterling Silver Plated |
|---|---|---|---|---|---|---|---|---|---|---|
| Aero | | x | | | | | | x | | |
| Americana Classic | | x | x | x | x | | | | x | |
| Atlas | x | | x | x | x | x | | | x | |
| Barron | | x | x | x | | | | x | x | x |
| Bolt Action Pen | x | | | | | | x | x | | |
| Bullet Pens | x | | | | | | x | x | | |
| Cambridge | | | x | | | | | | | x |
| Carbara | | x | x | x | | x | | x | | |
| Churchill | | x | x | | | | | | | x |
| Cigar Style | x | x | x | x | x | | | | x | |
| Classic Rollerball | x | | x | | | x | | | | |
| Click Pen | x | x | x | x | x | | | | | |
| Comfort pen | x | | x | x | x | x | | | x | |
| El Grande | | x | x | X | | | | x | | x |
| El Presidente | | x | x | | | | | | | X |
| Elegant Beauty | | | x | x | | | | x | x | |
| European Style | x | x | x | x | x | x | | | x | |
| Executive | x | | | | x | | | | | |
| Flat Top American | | | x | | | | | | | x |
| Gatsby | x | | x | | | | x | | x | |
| Gentleman's | | x | x | x | | | | | x | |
| Gran Torino | | | | | | | | | x | |
| Havana Pen | | x | | | | | | | x | |
| Ligero | | x | | | | | | | x | |
| Majestic | | | | | | | | | | |
| Majestic Squire | | | x | | | | x | x | x | |
| Navigator | x | | x | x | | | | x | x | x |
| Olympian | x | | x | | | | | | x | |
| Panache | | x | | | | | | x | x | |
| Phoenix | x | | | | | | | x | | |
| Polaris | x | | x | x | x | | | | x | |
| Premiso | | | | | | | | x | | |
| Princeton | | | x | x | | | | x | x | |
| Rinehart | | | x | | | | | x | | |
| Sedona | | | x | | | | | x | x | |
| Sierra | | | | | | | | | | |
| Slimline | x | x | x | x | x | x | | x | x | |
| Statesman's | | | | | | | | | x | |
| Triton | | x | | | | | | x | | |
| Tycoon | x | | | | | | | | x | |
| Venus | | x | | x | | | | | x | |
| Vertex magnetic | | | | | x | | x | x | | |
| Wallstreet II & III | x | x | x | x | | | | | x | |
| Zen—magnetic | | x | | x | | | | x | | |

# Plating

Current suppliers of pen kits offer at least a dozen different varieties of pen kit platings. Choosing the correct plating to match a particular pen blank can be a daunting task, but, in the next few sections, we will discuss some of the different platings that are currently offered and discover the pros and cons of each plating type.

When selling your latest pen creation, the combination of the material for the pen blank and the pen plating can make or break a sale. A general rule of thumb is to combine the plating that looks best with a contrasting pen blank. However, everyone's taste is different and just because you like a certain combination does not necessarily mean that the purchasing public will like what you like. My harshest critic—my wife—has on occasion informed me that a pen I made was "butt ugly" (my words, not hers), but even those pens have sold over time. That just goes to prove that there is a pen for everyone!

**Figure 3.5.** Can you tell the difference in plating by just appearance alone? The slimline pen on top is made from 24-karat plating, and the one on the bottom is the titanium nitride plating.

## 24-Karat Gold Plating

All of the current manufacturers of pen kits offer 24-karat (kt.) gold plating (see **Figure 3.5**). This is the entry level and least expensive of the platings. And what the old adage says, "You get what you pay for," definitely holds true here.

When exposed to constant abrasion, 24-karat gold plating is not durable. Abrasion can be an occurrence as simple as someone's fingers rubbing the plating and causing scratches as he or she uses the pen. Scratches also emerge when a pen is placed in and out of a pocket day after day, when a pen is tossed into a drawer (who would do that to a fine writing instrument?), or when a pen resides at the bottom of a purse.

However, it is not all doom and gloom for the 24-karat gold plating. Manufacturers can make the gold plating more durable depending on the method used in plating the material or by adding certain additives when they are plating the pen parts. In addition, the manufacturer can apply a topcoat of epoxy to the plating to prevent the finish from wearing off. It is difficult to determine exactly which gold plating is on the pen, so make sure that when you purchase the pen kit you inquire about exactly what type of gold plating you have purchased.

**Figure 3.6.** Platings that use titanium gold often feature a hallmark on the pen clip, like the one shown here.

**Figure 3.7.** Rose gold plating: The flat-top American-style pen on top is turned from figured eucalyptus; on the bottom is sycamore burl.

**Figure 3.8.** Black titanium plating: The Olympia pen on top is stabilized box elder burl, and the bottom pen is made from figured mesquite wood.

## Titanium Gold

The most durable and longest-lasting gold finish is titanium plating. This finish produces an extremely hard and durable gold finish. One manufacturer pioneered and uses a process that is called particle vapor deposition (PVD) when plating a titanium gold finish on its pen parts. Titanium oxide is matched to the color of the gold and is molecularly bonded to the pen part; then, 24-karat gold is bonded onto the pen part to achieve a color match. The final result is plating that will virtually never show wear and will always retain the glowing gold finish.

Simply by looking at the pens, it is difficult to distinguish the 24-karat gold plating from the titanium nitride plating. Some manufacturers place a hallmark on the clip of their pens to distinguish a TN pen from any other gold plating (see **Figure 3.6**).

## 18-Karat Swiss Rose Gold

This unique and rare plating combines copper and gold together in such a way that they both plate with their atoms equally mixed together (see **Figure 3.7**). The parts to be plated are specially treated before plating, and thus the plating is deposited in a very thick layer, producing an attractive and durable pen part. Because there is copper in the alloy, it may cause the Swiss Rose Gold to slightly tarnish. If this happens, the rose gold's luster can be brought back to the original shine by lightly buffing the surface.

## Black Titanium

This is a titanium oxide that is again molecularly bonded by the PVD process. This plating is unbelievably hard and durable, is much tougher than titanium nitride, and will last for many years (see **Figure 3.8**).

## Platinum

Platinum is a very durable, hard plating material, and one manufacturer uses real platinum rather than rhodium (see **Figure 3.9**). This plating can be expected to last for many years under normal, careful use.

## Sterling Silver

Parts that are plated with sterling silver receive a restaurant-grade 20-micron plating, which is very durable, to ensure that the beauty on the sterling silver lasts for many years (see **Figure 3.10**).

## Rhodium

Rhodium is a member of the platinum precious metal family but has unmatched brilliance and durability. Many manufacturers in the jewelry industry use rhodium to plate their fine jewelry pieces. Some of the world's premier pen manufacturers even use rhodium to plate their very finest pens (see **Figure 3.11**). Almost all of the current pen manufacturers guarantee their rhodium finishes for life.

## Satin Finish

This particular plating offers a unique alternative to traditional plating, and satin finish pens undergo a special plating process that produces a matte-like finish. The final product features a slight texture that looks and feels great (see **Figure 3.12**). This plating is durable and will last a long time.

## Chrome

This durable plating under normal use should hold up for many years. I like to match darker woods with chrome plating (see **Figure 3.13**).

## Black Chrome

Black chrome is also very durable and offers an alternative to traditional chrome plating. It works extremely well with lighter-colored woods (see **Figure 3.14**).

**Figure 3.9.** Platinum plating: From top to bottom, these El Grande pens are made from afzilia burl, black and white ebony, amboyna burl, and desert ironwood.

**Figure 3.10.** Sterling silver plating: The Churchill pen on top is stabilized spalted hackberry, and the bottom pen is stabilized buckeye burl.

**Figure 3.11.** Rhodium plating: The top pen is a gentleman's pen, made from axis deer antler, and the bottom is a closed-end Little Havana pen from rusa deer antler.

**Figure 3.12.** Satin finish: The executive ballpoint pen on top is Madagascar ebony, and the bottom pen is dyed and stabilized red maple burl.

**Figure 3.13.** Chrome plating: The top sierra pen is spalted English beech; the bottom pen is made from black ash burl.

**Figure 3.14.** Black chrome plating: This patriot pen is made from a redwood burl.

# CHAPTER 4

# Pen Blank Preparation

Once you select your pen plating, pen style, and pen blank material, it is time to prepare your blank for turning. The method of preparing a pen blank is the same no matter what material you are using.

**Figure 4.1.** Pen kits include all of the hardware you'll need to make a pen.

**Figure 4.2.** Use the tubes to correctly measure and mark the pen blank.

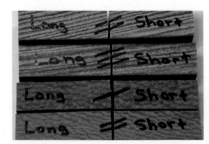

**Figure 4.3.** Avoid confusion by labeling the pen blanks clearly.

**Figure 4.4.** A simple stand such as this will keep pen blanks in order.

## Gather your materials

Open the pen kit and arrange the parts as per the instructions for the kit (see **Figure 4.1**). Most pen blanks will be at least ½" to ¾" square and 5" to 5¼" long. Each pen kit gives you the exact dimensions you will need for that particular pen blank. A quick way to measure this is to remove the pen tubes, place them on the material of your choice, and then cut them to the proper length, adding approximately ¹⁄₁₆" to each end (see **Figure 4.2**).

## Matching the pen blank

Once you cut your pen blank into two pieces, you will have to keep track of which end will be the top half of your pen and which end will be the bottom half of your pen (see **Figure 4.3**). Before you cut the blank in two, place orientation marks on the blank. If you are making more than one pen, mark each blank with its own designation. In Figure 4.3, note that the bocote pen blank on top is cut on an angle, whereas the bottom blank is cut with the grain running parallel. Both blanks have distinctive marks. A rubber band can be used to keep multiple pen blanks together, or you can make a holder by using holes drilled into a square piece of wood or Corian with dowels placed in the holes (see **Figure 4.4**).

# Drilling the pen blank

Holding a pen blank by hand and trying to drill straight through at a 90-degree angle is difficult, if not impossible. The best way to drill your pen blank is to use a pen drilling vise (**Figure 4.5**) or a drill chuck (**Figure 4.6**). The blank is placed into a pen vise for two main reasons. The first is to precisely drill the blank, and the second is to minimize the wandering effect of the drill bit.

First, make an *X* by drawing diagonal lines from corner to corner; the middle of the *X* will be the exact center of the pen blank (see **Figure 4.7**). Then, insert the blank into the pen vise. Drill at the exact center using a continuous speed and a slight downward pressure. Relieve the debris from the blank often. This will ensure the greatest chance of a clean and straight bore.

Problems can occur when too much pressure is applied and the debris is not removed often. This allows excessive heat to build up inside the pen blank. When excessive heat builds up too rapidly, it will cause a blowout, as shown in **Figure 4.8**. This problem can occur in both wood and acrylics.

Sometimes a blowout is the result of either a dull drill bit or an incorrect bit. When this occurs, more pressure is usually applied to the pen blank causing more heat to be generated, thus causing a blowout to occur.

The simplest way to avoid blow-out is to use a good-quality drill bit. I recommend two styles: the first is a good quality Norseman high-speed drill bit, and the second is the newest type of drill bit, the Colt parabolic drill bit (**Figure 4.9**). The Colt drill bits are made with M2 high-speed steel. Coupling the M2 HSS with the parabolic flute design, it will remove chips quickly and leave straight and clean holes in your pen blanks.

**Figure 4.5.** A pen-drilling vise used on a drill press will ensure an accurately drilled hole.

**Figure 4.6.** A drill chuck on the lathe can drill an accurate hole in the blank.

**Figure 4.7.** A simple *X* drawn from corner to corner will help you to find the center of the blank.

**Figure 4.8.** Blowouts in wood and acrylic (shown here) are caused by excess heat while drilling, perhaps because of a dull bit.

**Figure 4.9.** Compare the cutting flutes on a high-speed drill bit, top, with the new Colt parabolic bit, bottom.

# Gluing the pen tubes into the pen blank

After the pen blank is drilled, the next step is to glue the pen tubes into the blanks. These tubes are always made of brass, and their function is to hold the pieces of the pen together.

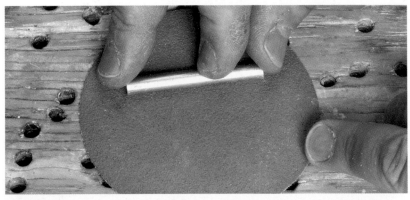

**Figure 4.10.** Rough up the tube by holding a piece of sandpaper still and rubbing the tube back and forth.

**Figure 4.11.** Apply thin CA glue to the inside of the wooden pen blank to give it added strength.

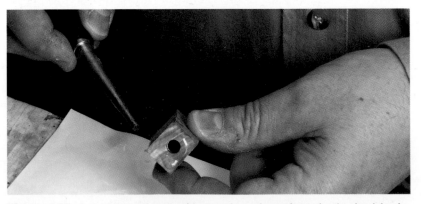

**Figure 4.12.** A pen insertion tool is used to place the tube in the blank.

Before the tubes are glued into place, the tubes have to be "roughed up" (see **Figure 4.10**). Take the tubes and rub them against a piece of 100-grit sandpaper to scratch them. This action gives the glue a better surface on which to adhere. Another method to rough up the tubes is to use a wire brush. A third method involves placing the pen tubes on a mandrel, then turning on the lathe while placing a piece of sandpaper against the tubes. Any method that scratches the brass tubes will suffice, so long as they are thoroughly scratched.

There are several types of glues that can be used to secure the tubes inside the pen blank. The two types used most often are cyanoacrylate (CA) glue (Super Glue belongs to this group) and epoxy. CA glue is offered in three thicknesses: The first is a very thick gap-filling type of glue, the next is a medium thickness, and the last is thin. The medium and thin CA glues are the most popular for pen making. (A word of caution about CA glue: It does not discriminate between wood and fingers.)

For non-stabilized wood pen blanks, the thin CA glue should be used first to coat the inside of the pen blank (see **Figure 4.11**). This is done for two reasons. If the wooden pen blank is porous, the thin CA glue gives the interior of the pen blank a better surface to which the medium CA glue can bond. It will also penetrate the wood blank, giving the finished pen additional strength. To apply the thin CA glue, allow several drops to fall into the hole in the pen blank as you turn the blank, allowing the CA glue to coat the inside of the pen blank. The above step (coating the inside of the pen blank with thin CA glue) is not necessary for any of the stabilized pen blanks or any acrylic or plastic material.

Place the pen tube on the pen insertion tool and pour some medium CA glue onto a piece of wax paper. A pen insertion tool helps insert the tube into the blank without getting glue all over your fingers. Coat the outside of the tube with the medium CA glue; then, insert the pen tube into one end of the pen blank, moving it in and out to coat at least one half of the inside of the blank. Now, reverse the tube and repeat the procedure on the other half of the pen blank. When you are finished, make sure that the pen tube is placed far enough inside the pen blank (see **Figure 4.12**). Repeat the process for the other half of the blank. You may choose to spray some CA accelerator on your pen blank at this time to speed up the drying time of your pen blank.

The preferred method of gluing green or wet wooden pen blanks is to use epoxy glues rather than CA glue (see **Figure 4.13**). The reason for the switch in glues is that the moisture inside the green pen blank sometimes accelerates the drying process of CA glue. The quick dry time will not allow you to place the tubes inside the pen blank to the proper depth before the glue dries. You will be stuck with the pen tubes not fully seated inside the pen blank (see **Figure 4.14**). The use of epoxy glues on not-yet-dry pen blanks will usually offer you more time to place the tubes into the pen blank. Follow the mixing instructions for the specific epoxy glue, and then use the guidelines as listed in the previous paragraphs to glue the pen tubes into the pen blank.

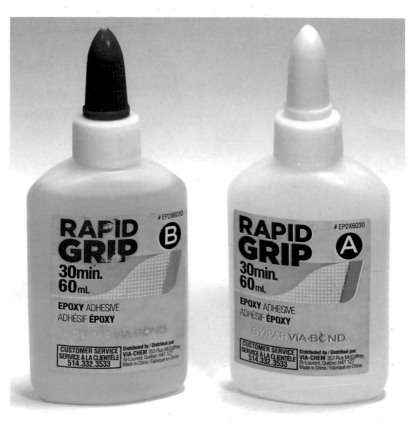

**Figure 4.13.** Two-part epoxy glue, not CA glue, is the best way to glue green or wet blanks.

**Figure 4.14.** CA glue dries too quickly in green wood blanks and can leave the tube seated incorrectly in the blank.

## Squaring the pen blank

Now that the tubes are glued into the pen blank, you must square the end of the pen blank in preparation for mounting the blank on a mandrel. Both ends of the pen blank must be square to the ends of the brass tubes inside the pen blank. This can be accomplished either by using a disc sander or using a special tool called a "pen mandrel," or a "barrel trimmer."

The easiest way to trim the ends of the tubes is with the use of the barrel trimmer (see **Figure 4.15**). Each particular pen kit will use a different barrel trimmer depending on the interior diameter of the pen tube.

By using a barrel trimmer of the appropriate size, two tasks will be accomplished. First, the inside of the pen tube will be cleaned of any glue that is present inside the tube; and, second, the end of the pen blank will be squared up to the barrel.

Use a pen vise or a chuck in the lathe headstock to firmly hold the pen blank, then square the ends of the tubes using a barrel trimmer attached to a portable hand drill (**Figure 4.16**). Completed properly, this operation makes the ends of the tubes slightly shiny, as shown in **Figure 4.17**. Be careful not to remove too much of the tubes, otherwise the pen will not assemble properly. Trim all the other ends of the tubes in the same way.

You'll need to make an adapter for pen kits larger than the standard 7 mm, 8 mm or 10 mm, as shown in **Figure 4.18**. Turn down an old mistake pen until it fits inside the larger pen tube, **Figure 4.19**.

As an alternative, you can use a disk sander to square the ends of pen tubes. Make a jig to hold the pen blank exactly square to the disk, as shown in **Figure 4.20**.

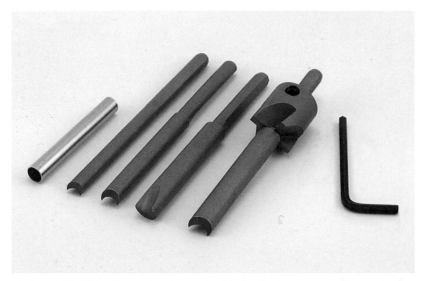

**Figure 4.15.** This photo shows a set of barrel-trimming tools ranging in size from 7mm to 10mm.

**Figure 4.16.** A drill-powered barrel trimmer cleans up a pen blank that's held in the lathe headstock (left), or held in the pen-drilling vise (right).

**Figure 4.17.** After the barrel trimmer has finished its job, the pen tube is clean, the excess wood has been removed, and the pen blank is now square. The next step is turning.

# Mounting your pen blank

Insert a mandrel into the headstock of your lathe. I have found over the years that it's best to only turn one half of the pen at a time. This way you will get a more concentric turning because you are working closer to the headstock of your lathe and you will encounter less wobble or whip from the mandrel. You can also use a mandrel saver and this will lessen the whip issue, as shown in **Figure 21**. Place the first section of your pen onto the mandrel, making sure that you have oriented the blank properly with the appropriate bushings for your pen kit. The bushings will guide you as to how much wood you should remove from the pen blank.

Once you have turned the wood down to the bushings so they are level, the pen has been turned to size. If you are using a mandrel saver, advance it over top of the mandrel until it rubs against the bushing and then lock down the tailstock. If you are not using a mandrel saver, then screw the locking nut onto the end of the mandrel, making sure that it is not put on too tightly. If you tighten the locking nut too tight, you may damage the mandrel rod and create a pen that is out of round. Snug the tailstock up onto the mandrel and make sure that you did not over-tighten the nut. The pen blank is now ready to be turned.

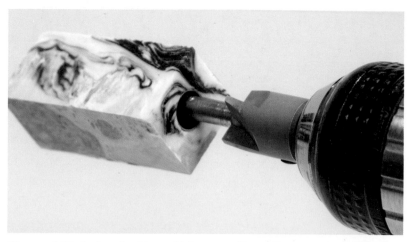

**Figure 4.18.** A standard barrel trimmer will not fit properly inside larger-diameter pen tubes.

**Figure 4.19.** Commercial metal and Delrin adapters are available, or you can make an adapter from a discarded pen so that the barrel trimmer will fit inside larger-diameter pen tubes.

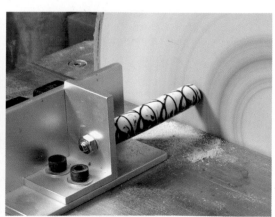

**Figure 4.20.** Rather than using a barrel trimmer, you can use a pen blank squaring jig and a disc sander to square the ends of your pen blanks.

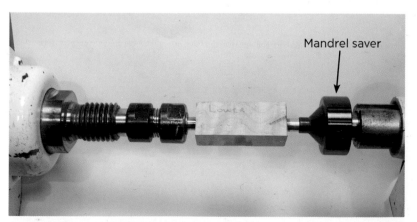

Mandrel saver

**Figure 4.21.** Mounting the pen blank with a mandrel saver will reduce the amount of whip and wobble.

# CHAPTER 5

# Pen Turning Tool Techniques

There are no "absolutely" correct ways to use pen turning tools as long as you do the fundamentals properly. I know I will get a lot of heat for that statement, but the reality is that, if you hold a skew with the long point (toe) down rather than up, make sure you have the tool resting on the tool rest, and make certain the bevel is rubbing the wood before you start to cut, you will be fine. These fundamentals will be covered in the next section, The ABC's of Tool Control. The idea is that you will be safe with the tools by using the ABC's.

## The ABC's of tool control

To turn the pens in this book, we'll be using a three-pronged approach to bevel cutting. You will obtain a much smoother cut by allowing the bevel of the tool to rub against the surface rather than by scraping the material.

The "A" stands for anchor. Make sure that your turning tool is firmly placed on the tool rest before contact is made with the pen blank. I know of no better way to catch a turner's immediate and undivided attention than seeing, hearing, and feeling a turning tool make contact with the material before it is firmly placed on the tool rest. Failing to secure the tool upon the tool rest prior to making contact with the wood will have a detrimental effect on you and possibly your pen blank. Hopefully you will only do that once or not at all!

The "B" stands for bevel. Confirm that only the bevel touches the surface of the material before you start cutting. If this does not occur, you will get an immediate "dig-in" and, once again, possibly ruin your pen blank.

The "C" stands for cut. Once the tool is anchored and only the bevel of the tool is touching the surface of the material, you can now slowly raise the handle of the tool to engage the surface of the material and proceed with the cut.

The ABC's described outline a procedure known as bevel cutting. Remember to put these principles in practice as we work through the next few pages.

## Speed of the lathe

Almost all pen blanks can be prepared with a lathe speed between 1500 and 2400 rpm. For pen blanks that are very large or irregularly shaped, such as deer antler (see **Figure 5.1**), you might want to slow down the lathe speed to approximately 600 to 800 rpm until the blank is rounded; at that time, the lathe speed can be increased to the higher speed listed above with no adverse effect on either you or the pen blank.

**Figure 5.1.** Slow down the lathe to 600–800 rpm when turning irregularly shaped blanks like the deer antler shown here. When the blank is rounded, speed up the lathe to its usual 1500–2400 rpm.

## Position the tool rest

Place the prepared pen blank on the mandrel with the bushings that are appropriate for the pen you are planning to turn. Ensure that your pen blank is properly oriented on the mandrel as indicated by the marks you made when you first cut your pen blank (see **Figure 5.2**). Adjust the tool rest height to approximately the center of the pen blank, as shown. It is important not to have the tool rest too high or too low with respect to the material you will be turning. If this occurs, the possibility of damaging your work is above average.

Rotate the hand wheel brake to make sure that the pen blank will not hit the tool rest (see **Figure 5.3**). If the blank does strike the tool rest, adjust the tool rest so you have about a ⅛" space between the pen blank and your tool rest. You do not want a large gap between the two because it increases your chances of jamming the turning tool between the tool rest and the pen blank, causing a serious catch or, worse, serious damage to the pen blank, the tool, or yourself (see **Figure 5.4**).

## Tool holding techniques

There are two ways to hold the turning tool. The first is the "underhand" technique. Note the position of the thumb (see **Figure 5.5**). It lightly holds down the top of the tool while your fingers support the tool from the bottom. Your other hand holds the back of the tool, waiting until you slowly raise the tool to make contact with the pen blank and start your cutting action. This technique can be done with either your left or your right hand.

The second way to hold a turning tool is called the "overhand" technique (see **Figure 5.6**). The hand in the foreground is firmly holding down the tool against the tool rest while the back hand is holding the tool, waiting to raise the tool up in order to make contact with the material.

The overhand technique is primarily used for turning larger objects, while the underhand technique is most widely used for turning pens and other smaller objects.

**Figure 5.2.** Following the directions in the pen kit you purchased, orient the blank and the bushings on the mandrel.

**Figure 5.3.** Turn the pen blank to ensure that the tool rest does not touch the pen blank.

**Figure 5.4.** If the tool rest is too far from the pen blank, the tool may catch between the blank and the rest.

**Figure 5.5.** In the underhand grip, the forefingers ride on the tool rest, and the thumb applies slight downward pressure on the roughing gouge.

**Figure 5.6.** The overhand tool grip is usually used when you are roughing out larger pieces.

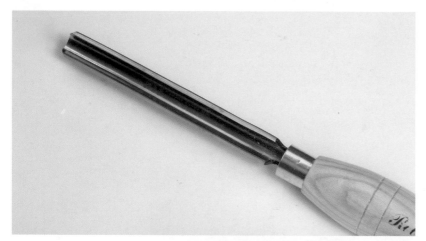

**Figure 5.7.** A roughing gouge is the first tool used when turning a pen. It removes the square corners of the blank.

**Figure 5.8.** The underhand technique and a roughing gouge are used here to remove the corners of the blank.

**Figure 5.9.** A roughing gouge and the bevel-rubbing technique, with side-to-side motion that removes surface wood, are used here to round the blank.

# Tools of the trade

Several basic tools are needed to turn pens. Let's take a closer look at the tools I'll be using to turn the pens in the step-by-step section of this book.

### Roughing Gouge

The first tool you will use to turn a pen will be a roughing gouge (see **Figures 5.7, 5.8, and 5.9**). This tool is used to cut away the square stock of your blank and turn it into a round cylinder. Again, note the position of the hand holding the roughing gouge; this is the underhand technique.

The roughing gouge is best utilized by placing the gouge firmly on the tool rest, part "A" of the turning ABC's. Then, advance the heel of the tool, which is the lower portion of the bevel, to come in contact with the wood, which is part "B." As the bevel of the gouge starts to make contact with the wood, slowly start to raise the handle of the tool, engaging the wood to obtain a clean cut on the surface of the material, which covers part "C."

## Skew Chisel

Because it is hard to get the bevel to come in contact with the wood properly, this tool strikes fear into the hearts of most turners who are just starting to learn the art of turning (see **Figures 5.10** and **5.11**). However, once you learn to properly use the skew, it will be your new best friend! Start by anchoring the skew on the tool rest—this is part "A." Slowly advance the skew until the bevel touches the surface of your material— part "B." Gently and slowly lift the handle of the skew until the center of the skew starts to cut the surface of the pen blank—part "C." If you do not present the bevel of the skew to pen blank properly, the result will be the dreaded "dig-in," or a large chip in the wood.

When you master the skew, you will be cutting with the center of the tool or the "sweet spot." The sweet spot on the skew is located in the center of the skew between the "toe," which is the upper portion, and the lower portion of the skew, called the "heel." When the tool is properly used, you will be rewarded with a superior finishing cut and with shavings, as shown.

## Spindle Gouge

Some turners like to put a bead or cove into some of their pens, while others do not. If you are going to turn any small objects other than pens, a small spindle gouge is a must (see **Figure 5.12**). Again, start as before with the gouge resting on the tool rest—part "A." Now advance the gouge into the work so just the heel of the bevel is slightly rubbing against the work—part "B." Now, slowly start to raise the handle of the gouge and roll the tool to the right—part "C." The flute of the tool should be facing away from the bead when finished. Do the same procedure to the opposite side to create a perfect bead.

**Figure 5.10.** A skew chisel, which can be an aggressive tool, is an important tool in a pen turner's toolbox. A dig-in (inset) will occur if the toe or the heel of the skew touches the pen blank before the bevel.

**Figure 5.11.** Note the clean shavings you can obtain by using the sweet spot of a skew chisel.

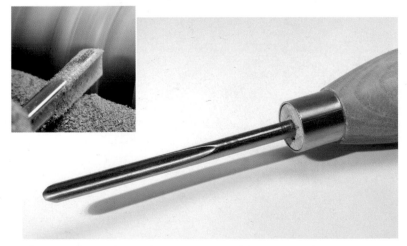

**Figure 5.12.** A ¼" spindle gouge is ideal for turning decorative beads and coves in your pens.

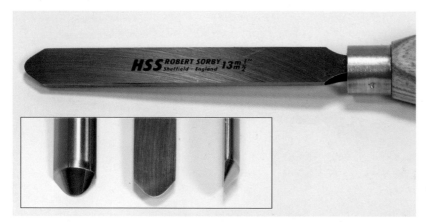

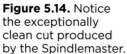

**Figure 5.13.**
The Spindlemaster
is a cross between
a skew and a
spindle gouge.

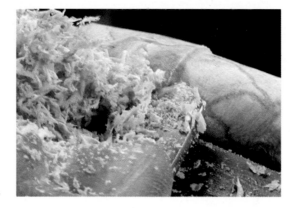

**Figure 5.14.** Notice
the exceptionally
clean cut produced
by the Spindlemaster.

## Spindlemaster

This unique tool is a cross between a skew and a spindle gouge. Its best advantage is that it takes the fear of using a skew out of the hands of the beginner. It can take the place of both a spindle gouge and a skew chisel (see **Figures 5.13** and **5.14**).

Place the Spindlemaster firmly on the tool rest before engaging it with the wood—part "A." Let the bevel come in contact with the surface—part "B." Slowly raise the handle of the tool to start cutting the material—part "C." Note how clean the surface becomes when the correct bevel-rubbing technique is applied. When the correct cut is attained, you will achieve shavings similar to the ones shown.

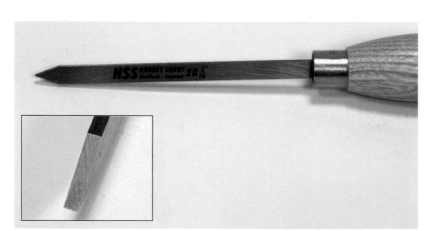

**Figure 5.15.**
A parting tool is
a useful tool for
special cuts.

**Figure 5.16.** Here, a parting tool
is used to cut a tenon on a blank.

## Parting Tool

The parting tool has many uses for general turning as well as specific uses for pen turning (see **Figures 5.15** and **5.16**). The parting tool should be held at a right angle to the surface you are cutting when you are using it in the bevel-rubbing mode. Note that the parting tool is anchored on the tool rest—part "A," the bevel of the tool is touching the pen blank—part "B," and when the handle of the tool is slowly raised, the cutting will commence—part "C." When these steps are properly completed, the parting tool will cut a clean tenon.

## Sandpaper

While sandpaper is not technically a tool, it can remove quite a bit of wood during the final stages of pen turning (see **Figure 5.17**). That's why, as you'll see later, I suggest that you don't turn a pen all the way down to the bushings before sanding. If you do, the sanding process may remove too much wood, making the wood of the pen lower than the bushings and creating a pen that won't assemble properly.

Most beginners will start sanding with 150-grit paper. Because the Spindlemaster makes a fine finish cut, starting with 220-grit sandpaper is possible. With practice using a skew, an even better finishing cut may be obtained thus allowing you to start with even higher grit sandpaper.

The sanding steps for beginners are as follows: 150 grit, 180 grit, 220 grit, 320 grit, 400 grit, 600 grit, and 800 grit. Sand lightly. Too much pressure will cause excessive heat, which will crack the pen. The 400-grit sandpaper will give a great finish. I usually take my pens to 4000 grit and even higher. I have found that the extra time—maybe one minute—that it takes to sand to this level is very small in comparison with getting a surface that has no micro-scratches.

As you add turning tools to your toolbox, remember to follow the ABC's of tool control, and you will be rewarded with many enjoyable hours of smooth, controlled cuts that turn beautiful pens.

**Figure 5.17.** I sand my pen blanks to 800 grit and then use Abralon sanding pads to 4000 grit. The Abralon pads are on top in 500, 1000, 2000, and 4000 grits. The bottom sandpaper is shown in 150, 180, 220, 320, 400, 600, and 800 grit.

# CHAPTER 6

# Dyeing and Staining

For hundreds of years, a desired finishing technique for furniture makers has been to change the color of the wood while allowing the grain patterns to be a visual part of their creations. It seems sacrilegious to take a highly figured, beautiful piece of tiger-striped or bird's-eye maple and artificially inject another color into the grain pattern, but that is exactly what will be accomplished in the following section. And the results are stunning.

Many different companies produce good-quality dyes and stains for wood. You must choose a stain that is correct for your particular application. For pen turning, a stain should be fade resistant, include ultraviolet protection, and dry quickly. Most importantly, the stain should not raise the grain. This is important because the stain is applied after the pen blank has been thoroughly sanded.

One other way to get dyed and stained wood is to purchase them commercially, such as stabilized and dyed pen blanks (see **Figure 6.1**).

## Aniline Dyes

Most turners are familiar with aniline dyes. Aniline dyes are fine powders that have to be dissolved in water, alcohol, or other solvents, depending on the formula (see **Figure 6.2**). Water-soluble aniline dyes are good for transparency of color and are easy to apply. The drawback with water-soluble dyes is that they may raise the grain, giving a fuzzy appearance to your project. The fuzzies can be removed, but this is another step one must complete. An alternative to the aniline dyes is alcohol-based stains.

## Alcohol-Based Stains

Alcohol-based, non-grain-raising dyes are known as NGR dyes (see **Figure 6.3**). Solar-Lux by Behlen is a non-grain-raising dye that is UV resistant. These dyes are used for several reasons. The stains that are offered can be used directly from the bottle, they may be mixed with each other to create other colors, and the translucency will enhance the pen blank's grain patterns. In other words, they are easy to mix, apply, and use to create unique grain patterns.

## A Word of Caution About Dyes

Avoid absorbing the dye through your skin and wear gloves when working with these dyes; they will stain your hands if protection is not worn. Make sure adequate ventilation is present and wear a mask. To avoid the possibility of spontaneous combustion, discard the application rags outside in a metal container.

**Figure 6.1.** Commercially available stabilized and dyed pen blanks come in a variety of colors.

**Figure 6.3.** Alcohol-based, non-grain-raising dyes like Solar-Lux by Behlen are UV resistant.

**Figure 6.2.** Fine-powdered aniline dyes can be dissolved in water, alcohol, or other solvents.

# DYEING THE PEN BLANK

1. Move the tool rest out of the way and thoroughly sand the pen blank to at least 800 grit or higher. Completely remove any dust that is present on the pen blank; if compressed air is available, use this to clean the pen blank.

2. Do not fill the grain or seal the wood; the stain must be able to penetrate the wood fibers.

3. Wearing protective gloves, pour a small amount of raw sienna (yellow) stain directly from the bottle onto a piece of cheesecloth (see **Figure 6.4**). While the pen blank is turning, lightly apply the stain to the pen blank. Make sure the blank is covered thoroughly.

4. Complete both halves of the blank (see **Figure 6.5**). Application of the stain should take no more than 15–20 seconds for both halves.

5. To apply a friction finish, immediately place a small amount of EEE cream on a clean piece of cheesecloth and remove the excess stain from the wood (see **Figure 6.6**). Continue to use the EEE cream for about 30–45 seconds.

6. After the EEE cream is applied, use woodturner's finish, such as Behlen's, on a paper towel and lightly apply the finish. Note how shiny the wood is and how much the grain stands out (see **Figure 6.7**).

7. Here is your finished pen with a friction finish (**Figure 6.8**).

**Figure 6.4.** Here, I am applying raw sienna with a piece of cheesecloth. Note the glove worn to protect my hand from the stain.

**Figure 6.5.** The stain has been applied full strength.

**Figure 6.6.** Remove the excess stain with EEE cream and a piece of cheesecloth.

**Figure 6.7.** Next I apply a woodturner's finish with a piece of paper towel.

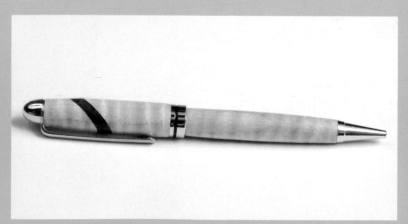
**Figure 6.8.** The finished pen. Raw sienna penetrated and enhanced the grain of the tiger-striped maple. The dark strip was cut from cocobolo.

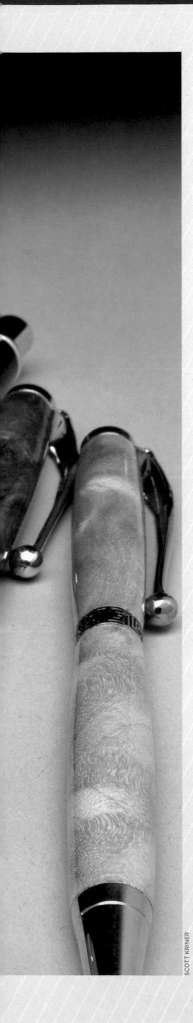

# PART 3

# Turning Wooden Pens

Now that you know the basics of pen turning, it is time to put your knowledge to the ultimate test: turning a pen in wood. In this section, you will learn step-by-step how to turn a slimline pen from a wooden pen blank, followed by two alternatives using the Slimline Pen kit. Every pen you make will involve the same steps as shown in the step-by-step section. Remember to think small when choosing interesting wood for your blanks and to follow the ABC's of turning as you proceed. Following the step-by-step section, there are four additional projects that can be made in any number of different materials.

SCOTT KRINER

Wood gives these fine pens a special richness.

# PROJECT 1
# Slimline Pen

The slimline pen uses a standard 7mm mandrel, 7mm bushings, and a 7mm drill bit. The plain band used in the demonstration can be switched out for a more ornate band, as shown below. The blank for this pen was cut from a maple burl growing in the forests of Virginia.

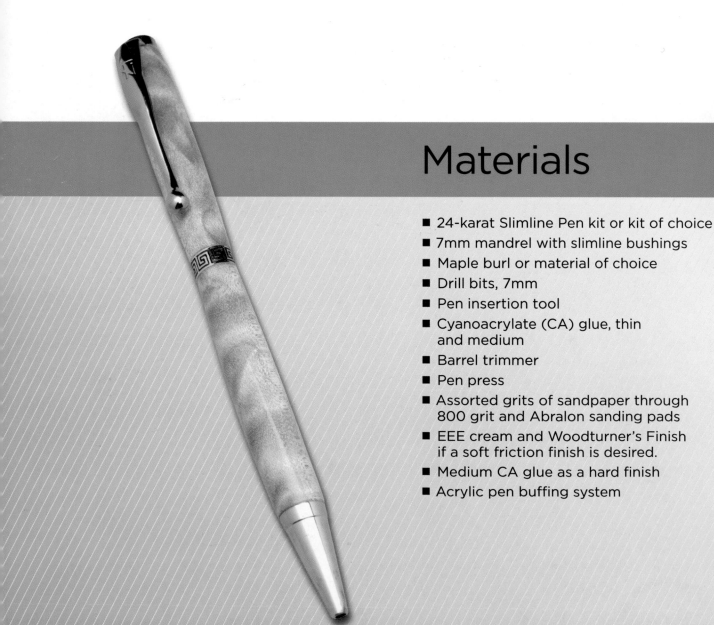

# Materials

- 24-karat Slimline Pen kit or kit of choice
- 7mm mandrel with slimline bushings
- Maple burl or material of choice
- Drill bits, 7mm
- Pen insertion tool
- Cyanoacrylate (CA) glue, thin and medium
- Barrel trimmer
- Pen press
- Assorted grits of sandpaper through 800 grit and Abralon sanding pads
- EEE cream and Woodturner's Finish if a soft friction finish is desired.
- Medium CA glue as a hard finish
- Acrylic pen buffing system

# Prepare the pen blank

For your first pen turning experience, why not make a dramatic statement by using a burl of your choice. When selecting a pen blank, think of the old adage "you can't judge a book by its cover," and you will do just fine. Just because the outside of a blank looks twisted and terrible doesn't mean that it won't make a beautiful pen. Try to visualize what the inside will look like. As you gain experience, you will be able to look at a piece of wood and see the highly figured pen inside!

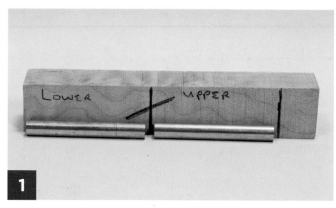

**1**

Mark the pen blank to size by using the pen tubes as a guide. Note the orientation marks on the blank. An extra 1⁄16" minimum was left on each end of the blank to allow for drilling.

**2**

Find the center of each piece of the blank by drawing a line from corner to corner, as shown.

**3**

Place the pen blank into the drill chuck and drill it with a speed of approximately 800–1000 RPM. Relieve the blank often to remove chips and to avoid heat buildup, which could cause the end of the pen blank to blow out.

**4**

Rough up the tubes by rubbing them against a piece of 100-grit sandpaper.

**5**

Note that the tube on the left has been roughed up; the tube on the right has not.

**6** On non-stabilized wood, coat the inside with thin CA glue. It will penetrate the wood and give the medium CA glue a good surface to stick to.

**7** An alternative to CA glue is 5-minute epoxy. If you use 5-minute epoxy, you will have to wait at least 10 minutes before starting to turn the blank.

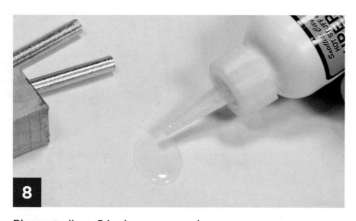

**8** Place medium CA glue on waxed paper.

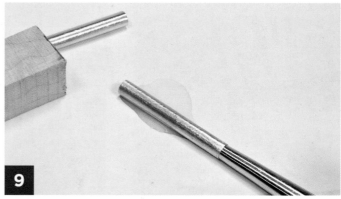

**9** Place the pen tube on the insertion tool, and cover the tube in the medium CA glue to coat the outside of the tube.

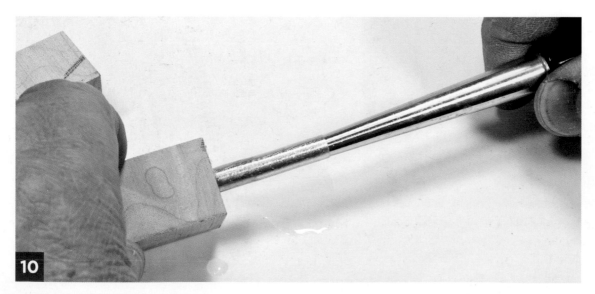

**10** Insert the tube into one end of the pen blank and go in and out to coat one half of the inside of the blank.

**11** Remove the tube and roll it in medium CA glue again. Reinsert it into the other end of the pen blank, and move it in and out again to coat the other half.

**12** When the inside of both halves of the blank are covered with glue, insert the tube to just inside the end of the pen blank, as shown.

**13** Square the ends of the pen blank using a pen mill. The pen mill can be driven by a portable drill with the blank held in a vise. Caution—Do not hand-hold the blank!

**14** A pen-drilling vise may also be used to secure the blank while the ends are being squared up.

**15** The disk sander with a squaring jig offers another way to square the ends of your pen blanks.

**16** Note how the end is square with the pen blank and the brass tube. Complete all of the steps for the other half of the blank.

# Turning the slimline pen

The shape of a slimline pen can be anything from straight across to slightly flared in the middle to any shape you want. Remember, it is your pen—you can turn beads, coves, captured rings, and any decoration you want. Given all of the shapes you can make, I have found, after making many pens, that the shape my customers like best has a slight flare in the center of the pen. This is only my suggestion, and you are the one making the pen, so enjoy yourself and make it the way you want!

Place the adjustable mandrel into the headstock followed by the appropriate bushing (7mm) for the Slimline pen kit, your pen blank, and the other 7mm bushing, then slide the mandrel saver over the mandrel rod and snug it against the bushing.

If you are not using a mandrel saver, place the adjustable mandrel into the headstock followed by the appropriate bushing (7mm for the Slimline pen kit), your pen blank, and the other 7mm bushing, and then thread the lock nut onto the mandrel shaft. Make sure you do not over-tighten the nut, which would cause the mandrel to bow slightly and possibly create an out-of-round pen blank.

Bring the tailstock with a live center up to the mandrel and lock it down. (A live center revolves and does not need to be lubricated.) Again, do not place too much pressure on the mandrel from the tailstock. Use the roughing gouge to round over the pen blank.

Continue the light rubbing process as more chips start to fly.

As the blank becomes more round, apply slightly more pressure with your back hand to cut more wood.

Once the blank is round you can switch your tool from a roughing gouge to a Spindlemaster to start to give your blank some shape. Note the clean finish you can achieve with bevel-rubbing techniques.

At this point you'll need to adjust your tool rest to keep it approximately ⅛" from your pen blank.

Continue using the Spindlemaster to create some final shape.

Use a skew in the bevel rubbing fashion to get smooth shavings

When you have reduced the pen blank slightly proud of the bushings, turn the lathe off, loosen the tailstock, and rotate the pen blank on the bushings; then re-tighten the tailstock. This will create a "new" center.

Take the skew and lightly touch just the ends of the pen blanks closest to the bushings. If your pen blank was out of round, this will remove that slight out of roundness and you will have a smoother blank at the ends of the bushings, giving you a better fit on your pen.

## Sanding the pen blank

Before you begin to sand the pen blank, take note of these few items. First, the sandpaper should be coming in contact with the pen on the bottom of the blank at approximately the 7 o'clock position. Second, check that adequate suction is being generated by the dust collection system to draw the dust being produced into the dust hood. Make sure that you are wearing your dust mask. Third, move the tool rest aside to facilitate the sanding process.

Once you have the desired shape, leave the blank slightly proud of the bushings. In other words, do not make the pen blank flush with the bushings at this time. If you do, when you sand the blank, the wood will be lower than the bushings, and, when you assemble the pen, you won't have a good fit.

## Applying a CA glue finish

Using cyanoacrylate (CA) glue as a finish will provide a very long lasting shine that is impervious to oily and sweaty hands and affords better scratch protection for your fine writing instrument. Personally, I have switched over to a CA glue finish for all my pens unless the customer specifically asks for a softer look; then, I give them a friction finish. My method to apply a CA glue finish is very easy and simple. After wet-sanding the hardened CA (Step 32), use the acrylic pen buffing system to give your pen blank a superior scratch-free shine.

Sand the blank to 800 grit, using 150, 180, 220, 320, 400, 600 and 800. After that, use the four Abralon pads (500, 1,000, 2,000 and 4,000) to finish the sanding process.

Protect your finger inside an empty parts bag and use a folded up paper towel to apply the CA glue. Place a liberal amount of medium CA glue onto the paper towel. Run the lathe around 100 rpm or spin the hand wheel by hand. Move the paper towel quickly back and forth across the pen blank. Remove the towel when you feel it getting sticky.

Use the aerosol spray accelerator to speed up the drying process and then place another load of medium CA glue to the pen blank, always moving back and forth. Apply 4 to 6 heavy coats, using the accelerator between coats.

Hand-sand any high spots to 320 grit. If you got glue on the bushings, use a parting tool to just lightly touch the ends of the bushings, to break the glue bond with your pen blank. Wet-sand the blank with acrylic sanding pads.

## Applying a friction finish

There are tons of products and techniques for finishing pens, but after trying many of them I have boiled finishing down to two choices: the CA glue finish and the friction finish using EEE cream and Behlen's Woodturner's Finish. The CA finish is harder and more scratch-resistant; the friction finish has a softer gleam to it.

Use compressed air to blow off any dust that is left after the sanding process.

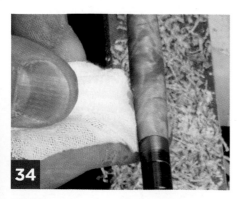

Rub the EEE cream back and forth on the bottom edge of your blank. As you are moving back and forth, a slight amount of heat is being generated. This is normal.

Once the EEE cream has been applied, use woodturner's finish, applied with a piece of paper towel.

With the woodturner's finish on a paper towel, apply light pressure under the blank, moving back and forth slowly. As the finish starts to dry, slowly start to put more pressure on the wood. The paper towel will become hot as the friction seals in the shine.

## Assembling the pen

A pen press, arbor press, drill press, or simply a vise can be used to assemble your pen blanks. The key to success is to make sure that the parts are aligned properly when pressing them together. If the pen parts are not pressed in correctly, you may crack the pen blank, so take your time when assembling your pen.

Remove the blanks from the mandrel, taking care to keep them in the same orientation that you turned them, and place them aside for assembly on an assembly rack.

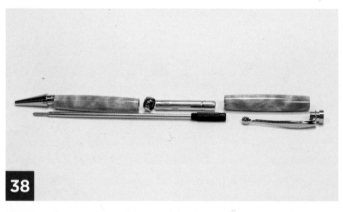

Line up the parts on the pen blanks, as shown and per the kit instructions.

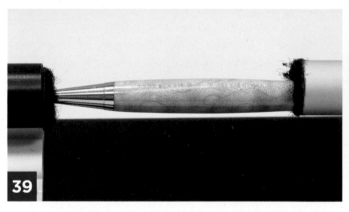

Start with the nib of the pen and press it into the front end of the blank.

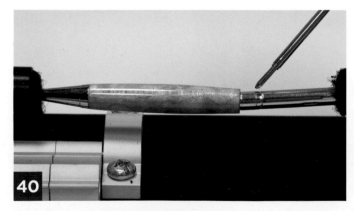

Press the twist mechanism into the pen to the mark on the line, as shown. Also note that the mechanism should not be going in on an angle, as shown. The severe angle may cause the end of the pen to split!

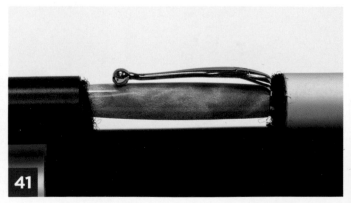

Next, press the top cap and clip into the top tube.

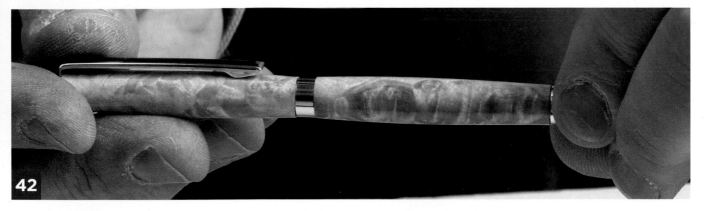

**42**

Place the band over the twist mechanism, and push the top section into the bottom section.

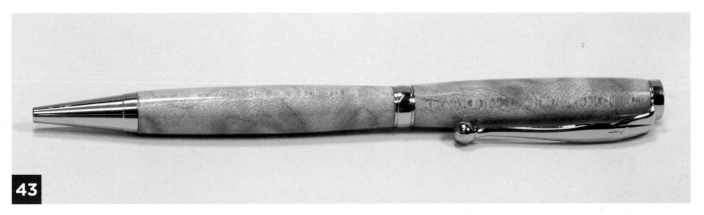

**43**

Here is your finished pen. Congratulations!

**44**

If you want a little variation, try putting a different center band on your pen.

## PROJECT 2
# Wire-Burned-Band Slimline Pen

The slimline pen has taken a lot of heat about being the entry-level pen. However, with a little creativity you can use this little pen and generate some variations that are very interesting and that may potentially increase your sales.

Creating a wire burning at the end of the upper barrel is easy to do, and it accents the pen in a positive fashion. For this project, we'll be making the center of the slimline pen fatter—and therefore changing the general shape of the pen—so we'll further differentiate this slimline pen with a different center band.

## Materials

- TN-coated Slimline Pen kit or kit of choice
- 7mm mandrel with slimline bushings
- Maple burl or material of choice
- Drill bits, 7mm
- Pen insertion tool
- Cyanoacrylate (CA) glue, thin and medium
- Barrel trimmer
- Pen press
- Assorted grits of sandpaper through 800 grit and Abralon sanding pads
- EEE cream and Woodturner's Finish if a soft friction finish is desired.
- Medium CA glue as a hard finish
- Acrylic pen buffing system

**1** Simply extend the length of the lower pen blank when you are first cutting the pen blank (**A**). Extend the length by ¼", which is longer than the size of the center band.

**2** Trim the ends of the pen blank as you normally would, but leave the extra wood on the one end of the pen blank. The pen tube is recessed inside the pen blank. Use the barrel trimmer to trim just the wood, leaving the blank ¼" longer than the normal length (**B**).

**3** Place the blanks on a mandrel with the 7mm slimline bushings, and turn the blanks even with the bushings on the clip and tip ends, leaving the center section of the pen blanks larger than the bushings (**C**). The diameter of the lower barrel should be slightly smaller than the diameter of the upper barrel.

**4** Because you will not use the center band that came with the kit, a center band or decoration of some sort must be created. Use the very tip of a skew to score small lines at the end of the barrel, and then use wire burners to create the burned lines (**D**).

**5** Sand and finish your pen blank as previously demonstrated in Steps 28 to 36 on pages 58 and 59.

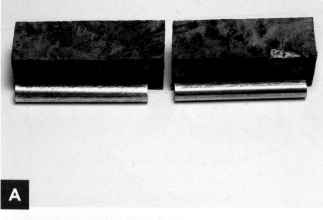

A

B

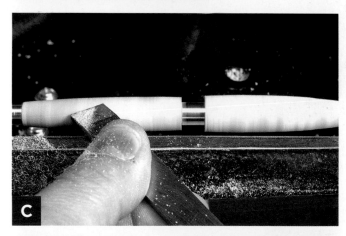

C

D

# PROJECT 3
# Corian Center-Banded Slimline Pen

This variation of the slimline pen in Project 1 is turned from a redwood burl and features a Corian center band. Start this project just as you did the wire-burned slimline by making the center portion of the slimline fatter. Using Corian as a center band gives this project a touch of color. You can also try using Color Grain or other dyed wood for the center band.

# Materials

- Rhodium-plated Slimline Pen kit or kit of choice
- 7mm mandrel with slimline bushings
- Redwood burl and a piece of Corian of choice or other materials of choice
- Drill bits, 7mm
- Pen insertion tool
- Cyanoacrylate (CA) glue, thin and medium
- Barrel trimmer
- Pen press
- Assorted grits of sandpaper through 800 grit and Abralon sanding pads
- EEE cream and Woodturner's Finish if a soft friction finish is desired.
- Medium CA glue as a hard finish
- Acrylic pen buffing system

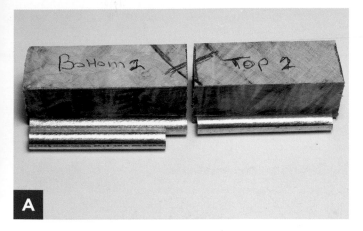

1. Use a longer 7mm tube from another pen kit **(A)**, such as a European-Style Pen kit, glue it into a pen blank, and square the ends.

2. Turn down the pen blanks as per Step 3 on page 63, but this time use a parting tool and remove ¼" from the end of the lower barrel. Make sure you have cut a square shoulder to assist in gluing the Corian piece to the end **(B)**.

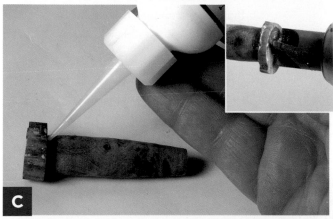

3. Use medium CA glue to glue the Corian piece to the end of the lower barrel. Then, trim the end of the lower barrel with a barrel trimmer **(C)**.

4. Continue to reduce the lower barrel using a skew **(D)** or a Spindlemaster.

5. Remove the center 7mm bushing and continue to reduce the blank until you have a smooth transition from the upper to the lower barrel **(E)**. Then, sand and finish the blanks as before in Steps 28 to 36 on pages 58 to 59.

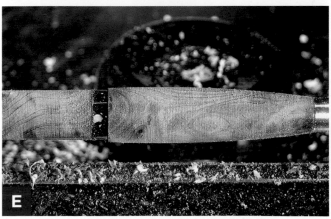

# Double-Dyed Buckeye Burl Comfort Pen

The popularity of the comfort pen makes this an admired style of pen and gives it an excellent track record for sales at craft fairs and shows. Shown here is a comfort pen turned from a piece of yellow and red double-dyed buckeye burl. The standard 7mm mandrel is used in conjunction with the comfort bushing set. Use two standard 7mm bushings, then the comfort bushing, followed by the lower blank, another comfort bushing, the upper blank, and a 7mm bushing.

## Materials

- Comfort Pen kit or kit of choice
- 7mm mandrel with comfort bushings
- Double dyed buckeye burl or material of choice
- Drill bits, 7mm
- Pen insertion tool
- Cyanoacrylate (CA) glue, thin and medium
- Barrel trimmer
- Pen press
- Assorted grits of sandpaper through 800 grit
- EEE cream and Woodturner's Finish for a soft friction finish.
- Medium CA glue as a hard finish
- Acrylic pen buffing system

PEN PHOTOGRAPH BY SCOTT KRINER

1  Cut the pen blank to the proper length and add 1/16" on each end (**A**).

2  Rough up the pen tubes by rubbing them on a piece of 100-grit sandpaper.

3  Drill the blank using a drill press and a 7mm Colt drill bit.

4  Glue the pen tubes into the blanks using thin CA glue, followed by medium CA glue. Use a twisting motion to spread the glue evenly inside the pen blank.

5  A 7mm barrel trimmer is used to square the ends of the blanks 90 degrees flush to the ends of the brass tubes (**B**).

6  Insert an adjustable mandrel into the lathe, place the nib-end comfort bushing on the mandrel followed by the lower pen blank, and add the center bushing for the comfort pen followed by either a mandrel saver or the locking nut for the mandrel.

7  Use the roughing gouge to start turning your pen. Continue to reduce the blanks using either the Spindlemaster or the skew to give the blanks the final shape just slightly proud of the bushings.

8  Because the comfort pen uses a soft gripper collar on the lower barrel, measure 1" from the end of the lower barrel and use a parting tool in bevel-rubbing mode to cut a clean shoulder. Remove wood down to the brass tube, then sand to 800 grit followed by the Abralon pads. Apply a CA finish on the lower portion and buff with the acrylic pen buffing system (**C**).

9  Turn the upper barrel down to the bushings, sand and apply a CA finish, and buff (**D**).

10  Line up all of the parts according to the instructions in the Comfort Pen kit and assemble your pen.

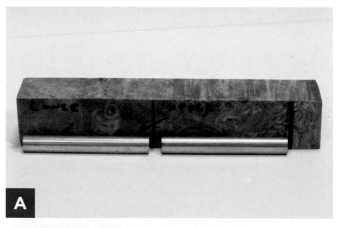

**A**

**B**

**C**

**D**

# PROJECT 5
# Acrywood Electra Rollerball Pen

All of the pen kits available on the market today that are a rollerball pen can be easily converted to a fountain pen, and vice-versa. The rollerball tip can merely be unscrewed and the spring and rollerball refill removed and replaced with a fountain pen tip and converter or cartridge. Making the rollerball pen and fountain pen are identical; you will shape the body of the pen, and the only difference is whether the rollerball tip or fountain pen nib is placed on the end of the pen. This project will shape the body of the pen and add the rollerball section. Because this is a combination of wood and acrylic material, we will apply a CA glue finish to the pen.

## Materials

- Electra rollerball pen kit or kit of your choice
- Acrywood black pearl pen blank or blank of your choice
- 7mm adjustable mandrel with Electra bushings
- Drill bit 10.5mm
- Pen insertion tool
- 5-minute epoxy to glue pen tubes
- Cyanoacrylate (CA) glue, medium, as a finish
- Barrel trimmer or squaring jig
- Pen Press
- Assorted grits of sandpaper to 800 grit
- Abralon finishing pads
- Acrylic pen buffing system

1  Cut the pen blank to the proper length and add ¹⁄₁₆" on each end. Then rough up the pen tubes for gluing by rubbing them on a piece of 100-grit sandpaper.

2  Drill the pen blank using the 10.5mm drill bit and drilling chuck (**A**).

3  Rough up the pen tubes and glue them into the barrel using 5 minute epoxy. Use a twisting motion to evenly spread the glue inside the pen blank (**B**).

4  Square the ends of the tube using a barrel trimmer or a squaring jig.

5  Insert the adjustable mandrel into the headstock of the lathe. Place the Electra bushings onto the mandrel as per kit instructions and then slide your blank onto the mandrel followed by the bushing.

6  Use a roughing gouge to start turning your blank and continue to reduce the blank down to the bushings using a Spindlemaster or a skew (**C**).

7  Sand the blank to 800 and then use the Abralon finishing pads. The Abralon will remove any micro scratches you might have on the blank.

8  Blow off the blank to remove any sanding dust and then apply the CA glue finish using the medium CA glue (**D**).

9  Wet-sand the CA glue finish and then buff with the acrylic pen buffing system.

10  After the blank is buffed and you are ready to assemble your pen, chamfer the inside edge of the blank to assist you in assembly (**E**). The chamfer helps align the pen parts with the body of the pen when you press them into place. Assemble your pen as per kit instructions and you now have a rollerball pen.

# Spalted Tiger Oak Gatsby Click Pen

While attending craft and pen shows, customers pick up this pen and the first thing they do is click it several times. Perhaps it is a nervous habit on their part or they are simply trying out the merchandise. Whatever the reason the click pen still has value and people do like the tactile feel of clicking their pens. This pen incorporates a Parker style refill that is readily available at any large office supply store. Any pen that uses a Parker style refill will offer you the opportunity to replace the standard ball point with a very smooth-writing ink gel refill because the smoother your pen writes, the easier it is for you to sell it.

## Materials

- Gatsby rhodium click pen kit or kit of your choice
- Spalted tiger oak pen blank or blank of your choice
- 7mm adjustable mandrel with Gatsby bushings
- Drill bit ²⁷⁄₆₄"
- Pen insertion tool
- 5-minute epoxy or medium CA glue to glue the pen tubes
- Cyanoacrylate (CA) glue, medium, as a finish
- Barrel trimmer or squaring jig
- Pen press
- Assorted grits of sandpaper to 800 grit
- Abralon finishing pads
- Acrylic sanding pads
- Acrylic pen buffing system

1. Measure the pen blank to the proper length and add ¹⁄₁₆" on each end. Cut the blanks; then, rough up the pen tubes by rubbing them on a piece of 100-grit sandpaper.

2. Drill the pen blank using a ²⁷⁄₆₄" drill bit and drilling vise.

3. Glue the pen tubes into the blank using a twisting motion to spread the glue evenly inside the pen blank.

4. Square the ends of the blank using a barrel trimmer or the squaring jig.

5. Insert the mandrel into the head stock and place the Gatsby bushings on the mandrel according to the pen kit instructions, followed by the pen blank and then the mandrel saver.

6. Using a roughing gouge, start turning your pen blank and continue to reduce it using either a Spindlemaster or a skew (**A**).

7. Move the tool rest out of the way, start sanding, continue up to 800 grit, and then use the Abralon pads. Blow off the sanding dust and apply a medium CA glue finish to your pen blank, then wet-sand using the acrylic sanding pads.

8. To assist in removing the pen blank from the bushings after applying CA glue, use a parting tool to just cut the glue off the bushings (**B**).

9. If, after removing the blank from the bushings, there is a little of the CA glue sticking up on the end of the barrel, carefully dip the ends of the pen blank in a drop of thin CA glue to harden the CA glue that is sticking up (**C**).

10. Once the CA glue hardens, use a nail file to sand the edge of the pen blank flat (**D**).

11. Buff your pen blank using the acrylic pen buffing system.

12. Assemble your pen according to the instructions for the Gatsby kit (**E**).

A

B

C

D

E

## PROJECT 7
# Lacewood Cigar Pen

These big, beefy, well-built pens are always a favorite at shows and craft fairs. Designed with strength and power in mind, the pen still fits in your hand with elegance and grace. This is a preferred pen for people who want to make a statement with their writing instrument. These pens are always a top seller with people who have a problem holding a smaller pen. Use the standard 7mm mandrel in conjunction with the cigar three-piece bushing set. The drill bit used in this demonstration is a 10mm brad point drill bit.

# Materials

- Cigar Pen kit or kit of choice
- 7mm mandrel with cigar bushings
- Lacewood or material of choice
- Drill bit, 10mm
- Pen insertion tool
- Cyanoacrylate (CA) glue, thin and medium
- Barrel trimmer
- Pen press
- Assorted grits of sandpaper through 800 grit and Abralon sanding pads
- EEE cream and woodturner's finish

1   Cut the pen blank to the proper length and add
    ¹⁄₁₆" on each end. Then, rough up the pen tubes by
    rubbing them on a piece of 100-grit sandpaper.

2   Drill the blank using a drill press and a 10mm brad
    point drill bit (**A**).

3   Glue the pen tubes into the blanks, first using
    thin CA glue, followed by medium CA glue. Use a
    twisting motion to spread the glue evenly inside the
    pen blank.

4   A 10mm barrel trimmer is used to square the ends
    of the blanks 90 degrees flush to the ends of the
    brass tubes.

5   Insert the mandrel into the headstock of the lathe
    and use the cigar bushings. Note that the blank will
    hit the tool rest if the lathe is turned on at this point
    (**B**). Check to be sure that the blank is clear before
    starting your lathe.

6   Use the roughing gouge to start turning your pen.
    Continue to reduce the blanks using the skew or
    Spindlemaster. The top barrel should have a slight
    taper toward the cap bushing.

7   Move the tool rest out of the way and start sanding
    your pen to a desired finish. I recommend sanding
    to at least 800 grit, followed by Abralon pads.

8   Using a piece of cheesecloth, apply EEE cream.
    Then, apply woodturner's finish on the turned
    blanks with a paper towel (**C**).

9   Assemble your pen according to the instructions
    in the Cigar Pen kit.

# PART 4

# Turning Pens from Other Materials

In addition to wood, there are a number of materials that can be turned on a mini-lathe. Any one of these materials can be made into an interesting and unique pen. In the following section, you'll learn step-by-step how to turn a cigar-style pen from Corian, a solid surface substance most often used in kitchen and vanity countertops. Five other projects, each using a different material—everything from acrylics to deer antler— follow the main demonstration.

These pens are made using an amazing range of natural and composite materials, as you'll see in this section.

# PROJECT 1
# Cigar Corian Pen

Corian comes in an assortment of colors, making it suitable for a variety of projects, including pens. Corian comes in three standard thicknesses—¼", which is used in bathrooms; ¾", which is used for commercial applications; and the most prevalent ½", which is used primarily for kitchens. Corian can be easily glued together to make the thicker pieces needed for larger pens. Let your imagination run wild with its uses, such as accent stripes in your wooden pens (see Project 4: Electra Acrywood Rollerball Pen on page 90).

Turning Corian is not difficult; you just need to keep your tools sharp. So, let's make some Corian dust and turn a pen!

## Materials

- Gold Cigar Pen kit or kit of choice
- 7mm mandrel with cigar bushings
- Corian of choice or other material of choice
- Drill bits, 10mm
- Pen insertion tool
- Clamps
- Cyanoacrylate (CA) glue, medium
- Barrel trimmer
- Pen press
- 220-grit sandpaper and acrylic pen finishing kit
- Acrylic pen buffing system

# Prepare the Corian pen blank

Turning Corian is just as easy as turning wood. When turning Corian, it is especially important that you start out with sharpened tools and keep them sharp throughout the turning process.

Corian comes in three different thicknesses. For pen making, the ½" size will serve our needs best because of the wide variety of colors offered. However, since most of the larger pens need a thicker pen blank of at least ⅝" to ¾",

the ½" material must be glued together to form a larger pen blank.

The first step will be to glue two pieces of Corian together so the glue line does not show after it is turned. There is nothing more frustrating than gluing pieces together, turning the blank, and then noticing that you can see the glue line. The method that follows will ensure that your glue lines will not be visible.

**1**

Corian has a good side, which is smoother than the back side. The back side may have writing on it. Cut two pieces of Corian ¾" x ¾" x 5¼". Wipe the good sides with ethyl alcohol and allow them to dry. Apply medium CA glue, rubbing the two pieces together. Before the glue dries, pull the pieces apart to see that the glue is evenly distributed.

**2**

Coat the good sides with medium thickness CA glue and clamp them together (**Note:** One clamp was removed for picture clarity.) Spray accelerator will speed up the drying process; however, wait at least 15 minutes for the glue to thoroughly cure.

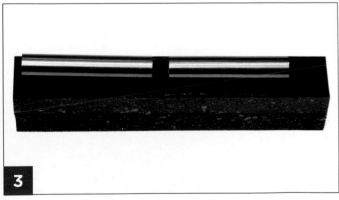

**3**

Place the pen tubes on the pen blank and add ¹⁄₁₆" to each end for proper length. Do not forget to mark which blank is the upper (short) blank and which is the lower (long) blank.

**4**

Cut the pen blank to the proper length. Use the pen tubes as a guide, as shown.

# Drilling the pen blanks

When drilling any acrylic material, such as Corian, use a high-speed twist drill bit rather than a brad point drill bit. A brad point drill bit may cause some chipping when exiting your pen blank and thus cause a blowout. In addition to using a sharp twist drill bit, relieving the debris often and not letting it build up inside the hole will also aid in preventing a blowout (see Figure 4.8 on page 37).

Place the cut pen blank into the pen vise and draw diagonal lines from corner to corner to find the exact center of the blank.

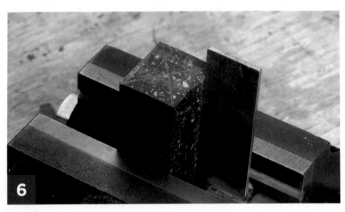

Use a small square to make sure that the pen blank is perpendicular to the drill bit.

Drill the blank using a drill press and a high-speed steel twist drill bit. The secret to drilling acrylic material is to make sure that you frequently remove drilled material from the blank.

As you get toward the end of the pen blank, lighten your touch on the drill so you will not have a blowout at the end. Blowouts are the result of too much heat building up because you are going too fast.

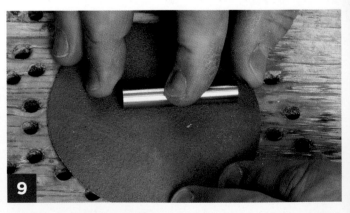

Scratch the surface of the pen tubes using a piece of 100-grit sandpaper. Scratching the surface will make the glue bond better with the surface.

Notice the tube on the left is for the lower blank. It has not yet been scratched. The tube on the right is for the upper blank. That one has been scratched.

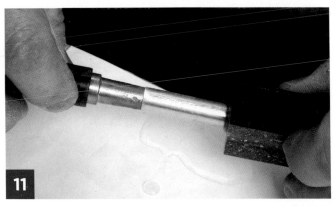

Glue the scratched tubes inside the drilled blanks. Place the longer tube on the insertion tool and roll the tube in CA glue. Place the tube into one end of the blank, rolling it around and going in and out of the hole. Repeat the same motion on the other end of the blank and insert the tube. Let it dry for 15 minutes. Complete the steps for both halves of the blank.

Hold the pen blank firmly with either a drilling chuck or a drill vise. Insert a 10mm barrel-trimming tool into a portable drill and slowly start to square up the ends of the tube so they are even with the end of the blank. The barrel-trimming tool will clean any CA glue from the inside of the tube. Use the pen vise to hold the pen blank while squaring the tube.

Trim the pen blank only to the end of the brass. **Important note:** If you trim too much of the blank away, the pieces will not fit together properly when you assemble the pen. (This potential problem is further addressed in Part 6, "FAQs and Troubleshooting," on page 121.)

## Turning the Corian pen blanks

The first rule in turning any acrylic material, such as Corian, is to use sharp tools. You are using a sharp drill bit when you are drilling the material, so you must use sharp turning tools to turn the blanks. When you begin roughing the material, take "light bites" with your tools. If you are too aggressive, you can cause large pieces of the acrylic material to tear out. (This potential problem is further addressed in Part 6, "FAQs and Troubleshooting," on page 121.)

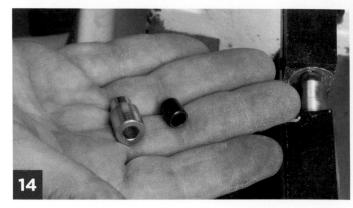

Place a 7mm spacer bushing on the mandrel. The front 10mm bushing is followed by the lower blank, then the center bushing, then the upper blank, and finally the top 10mm bushing and a 7mm spacer bushing. Note the size difference between the 7mm bushing on the right and the 10mm bushing on the left.

Insert the mandrel into the headstock of the lathe. Place the 10mm bushings on the mandrel with the smaller bushing in the front, followed by the center bushing, then the larger top bushing, as shown.

Move the tool rest up and center it, leaving approximately ⅛" between the tool rest and the pen blanks. Rotate the hand wheel to make sure that the blanks do not come in contact with the tool rest.

Using the roughing gouge in the bevel-rubbing mode, start to lightly rub against the blank, taking off little bits of the Corian at a time. Note the shavings coming off the blank.

Check for the roundness of the blank by placing the gouge on top of the blank, as shown. If you hear a "rap, rap, rap" sound, you know you still have to turn some more to make it round.

Continue to round over the blank. As you get the blank to a more rounded state, you will get longer streams of material coming off your gouge.

Remember, as the blank continues to get smaller, you must keep moving the tool rest closer to the blank. Now, you can start to apply more pressure on your tool and take deeper cuts in order to remove more material faster.

Once the blanks are round, the Spindlemaster can be used to start to shape the pen.

Notice the clean shavings from this tool and how the left hand is being used to turn the blank. Do not be afraid to use both hands. Once you learn to use your non-dominant hand, you will become a better turner.

As you get toward the desired shape, use a skew chisel to clean up the ends of the blank. Note how the sweet spot of the skew is used, and look at the fine shavings being generated.

Use a skew to clean up the lower blank and to give it the final shape you want. As with the wooden pen, leave the blank slightly proud of the bushings so you can sand it flush.

## Sanding and finishing your Corian pen

A quick note about sanding acrylic material: Padded aluminum oxide sanding pads have been used by the kitchen and bath industry for years to take away scratches on countertop surfaces. Because we are using the same material, Corian, why shouldn't we use this same technology to polish our pens to a scratch-free shine? The brightly colored aluminum oxide sanding pads can be used to quickly sand and polish your pen to a scratch-free shine. Use each successive pad for the same amount of time. Usually this is about 10 to 15 seconds per sanding pad.

Move the tool rest out of the way and sand the blank with 320-grit sandpaper until the blank is flush with the bushings.

Place a towel on the bed of the lathe to prevent the lathe from becoming wet. Start with the 800-grit, 2" x 2", green aluminum oxide pad from the acrylic pen finishing kit. Place a few drops of water on the pad and start to wet-sand the blank.

There will be a whitish slurry created by the aluminum oxide pads and the Corian surface. This is normal. In reality, you are polishing the blank with this slurry. Just wash off the pad and it can be used over and over again.

On each half of the blank, use the peach-colored aluminum oxide pad, which is 1500 grit. These pads are used wet with a gentle touch. If too much pressure is applied, the heat generated will cause the glue from the pad to come off on the blank.

Purple is the next color used, and it is 2400 grit.

Light blue, representing 4000 grit, is the next color. The blanks are becoming shiny, and all of the scratches are gone.

The final aluminum oxide sanding pad, gray in color, is 12000 grit. This will feel like nothing, but trust me, it is placing a shine on the material that you will not believe!

Buff your pen blanks starting with the blue rouge wheel followed by the white buffing wheel.

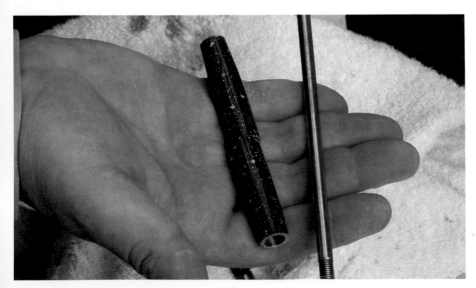

The entire wet sanding/polishing process, from the green pad to the gray pad followed by buffing, took less than three minutes to get this scratch-free shine!

## Assembling your Corian pen

Care must be taken when assembling your acrylic pen because the material on the edges of the pen blank may be less than ³⁄₆₄" thick. Therefore, make sure that you insert the pen pieces absolutely straight into the pen tubes. If you are just a bit off center, you may crack the acrylic material because it is so thin at the edges. A pen press alleviates this concern when assembling your pen.

**33**

Line up all of the parts by placing them into the pen, as shown.

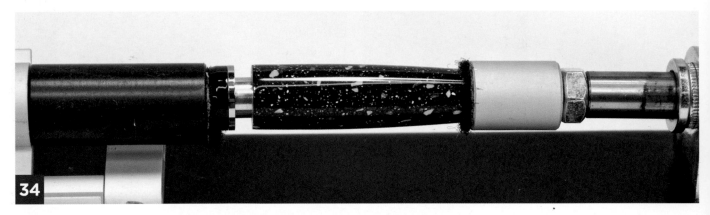

**34**

Place the gold disk on the center band. Press the center band into the lower portion of the upper tube.

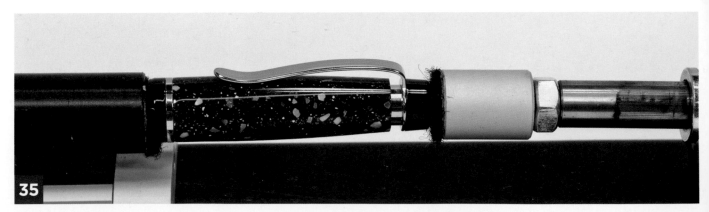

**35**

Insert the clip/coupler assembly into the upper portion of the top blank and press them together. The upper portion is complete.

Press the tip into the lower portion of the pen blank with the pen press.

Now press the center coupling into the other end of the lower blank.

Place the refill with the spring inside the lower barrel and screw the twist mechanism on the center coupling. Push the upper portion of the pen on to the lower portion, and now you have the rest of the pen. Do not be alarmed; the twist mechanism will turn both ways to open and close the pen.

## PROJECT 2

# Acrylic Scrap Sectional Gatsby Pen Turned Between Centers (TBC)

What do you do with all the leftover and cut-off scrap pieces of wood and acrylic that have accumulated all over the shop from making your pen blanks? You hate to throw away the cut-off pieces so you just keep saving and saving as the scrap pile keeps growing ever larger and larger. You can use some of them as accent pieces or inserts for pens but that still leaves a lot. Some time ago, while demonstrating at a woodworking show, a former student came up and showed me a pen he had made from all the scraps in his shop and ever since that time I have been showing students how to use all those scrap pieces. You knew that someday you would use them—well, that someday is now!

## Materials

- Gatsby rhodium pen kit or kit of your choice
- Any and all scrap material lying around the shop
- 60° Dead center (for headstock)
- 60° Live center (for tailstock)
- TBC Bushings for Gatsby Pen Kit
- Drill bit $^{27}/_{64}$"
- Pen Insertion Tool
- 5-minute epoxy or medium CA glue
- Barrel trimmer or squaring jig
- Pen Press
- 320-grit sandpaper
- Acrylic sanding pads
- Acrylic pen buffing system

1   Sand a number of scrap sections on a slight angle and glue them together using medium CA glue. Make sure that you glue up enough scrap to be slightly longer than the pen tube that you will use (**A**).

2   Use a disc sander to square the pen blank to make it easier to drill the hole for the pen tube (**B**).

3   Use a ²⁷⁄₆₄" drill bit and drill a hole through your blank using the drilling chuck or pen-drilling vise to hold your pen blank.

4   Rough up the pen tube with 100-grit sandpaper; paint the tube black just in case there is a gap in your gluing up of the pieces. Glue the pen tubes into the blank using a twisting motion to spread the glue evenly inside the hole (**C**).

5   Square the ends of the blank using a barrel trimmer or the squaring jig.

6   Insert a 60° dead center into the headstock of your lathe and a 60° live center into the tailstock. Place the special TBC bushings (which have a 60° indent to them) in the pen blank and place it in between the headstock and tailstock, applying a medium pressure (**D**).

7   Using a roughing gouge, start turning the pen blank; continue to reduce it down to the TBC bushings using either a Spindlemaster or a skew.

8   Move the tool rest out of the way and sand using only 320 grit to remove any tool marks.

9   Wet-sand with the acrylic sanding pads and then buff using the acrylic pen buffing system.

10   Assemble the pen according to the instructions for the Gatsby pen kit.

# Phoenix Cholla Cactus Pen

Single-barrel pens are very popular and easy to make and most single-barrel pen kits will allow you to get two pens from a single pen blank. Another popular idea is creating pens from recycled material. For this project, we will take dead cholla cactus, which has a naturally drilled hole in the center thanks to Mother Nature, and fill the voids with crushed turquoise or red coral.

## Materials

- Phoenix chrome pen kit or kit of your choice
- 7mm adjustable mandrel with phoenix bushings
- Drill bit $^{27}/_{64}$"
- Pen insertion tool
- Thin & medium cyanoacrylate (CA) glue
- Squaring jig with a disc sander
- Pen press
- Sandpaper to 800 grit
- Abralon pads
- Acrylic sanding pads
- Acrylic pen buffing system

PEN PHOTOGRAPH BY SCOTT KRINER

1 Add 1/16" to each end of a piece of cholla cactus blank and cut to the to the proper length using the pen tube as your guide (**A**).

2 Use a 27/64" drill bit and drill a hole into the center of your blank using the drill chuck or pen drilling vise to hold your cactus blank. You are not really drilling a new hole, just reaming out the existing hole that Mother Nature has provided (**B**).

3 Rough up the pen tube using 100-grit sandpaper and slide it into the cholla cactus. Do not glue the pen tube in at this time.

4 Commercially available crushed turquoise and other fillers such as red coral are readily available or you can crush your own (**C**).

5 With the pen tube inside the cactus (not glued in at this time yet), place some crushed turquoise inside just a few of the holes in the cactus and drip thin CA glue over the turquoise. Allow the thin CA glue to soak into the wood and turquoise (**D**). Just fill in a few of the holes and do not trim the ends of the blank with a barrel trimmer—it will tear your blank apart!

6 Insert an adjustable mandrel into the headstock of your lathe and place one of the Phoenix bushings onto the mandrel, followed by the cactus blank and then the other bushing and the mandrel saver or the brass nut on the mandrel.

7 Using a roughing gouge start turning your pen blank, continue to reduce it down close to the bushings using either a Spindlemaster or a skew. You will see voids in the cactus blank because you did not fill up every hole. The reason to not fill every hole in the beginning is, a lot of turquoise material would just be wasted turning it down to the bushings.

8 Remove the cactus blank from the mandrel and fill in any of the holes that have appeared and drip thin CA glue over the entire pen blank. Now use a disc sander and squaring jig to square up the pen blank.

9 Place the blank back onto the mandrel and turn the blank flush to the bushings. Move the tool rest out of the way, sand to 800 grit followed by the Abralon pads. Blow off the blank with air and then apply a medium CA finish as described on page 58.

10 Wet-sand with the acrylic sanding pads and then buff using the acrylic pen buffing system.

11 Assemble your pen blank according to the instructions for the Phoenix pen kit.

# PROJECT 4
# Electra Acrywood Rollerball Pen

This pen kit updates the American classic flat top pen kit by using a new material for turning, Acrywood. Acrywood combines acrylic and wood together in one pen blank. Burl caps from maple, box elder, or other light-colored woods are combined with vibrant resins to form these unique, one-of-a-kind nature-inspired pen blanks. This type of kit is so popular because it can be easily upgraded to a fountain pen by simply unscrewing the rollerball tip and replacing it with a fountain pen nib.

## Materials

- Electra upgrade gold & chrome pen kit or kit of your choice
- 7mm adjustable mandrel with Electra bushings
- Drill bit 10.5mm
- Pen insertion tool
- 5-minute epoxy
- Medium cyanoacrylate (CA) glue
- Barrel trimmer or squaring jig
- Pen press
- Sandpaper to 800 grit
- Abralon pads
- Acrylic sanding pads
- Acrylic pen buffing system

**1** Add ⅟₁₆" to each end of a piece of Acrywood blank and cut to the to the proper length using the pen tube as your guide.

**2** Use a 10.5mm drill bit and drill a hole into the center of your Acrywood pen blank.

**3** Rough up the pen tube using 100-grit sandpaper and glue the pen tube into the blank using 5-minute epoxy (**A**).

**4** Use a barrel trimmer or a squaring jig to square the ends of the pen blank.

**5** Insert an adjustable mandrel into the headstock of your lathe and place one of the Electra bushings onto the mandrel, followed by the Acrywood blank, then the other bushing, and then the mandrel saver.

**6** Using a roughing gouge, start turning your pen blank, and continue to reduce it down close to the bushings using either a Spindlemaster or a skew. Turn the lathe off, loosen the tailstock to rotate the bushings, and then re-tighten the tailstock and finish turning the blank down to the bushings.

**7** Sand the blank to 800 grit followed by the Abralon pads.

**8** Blow off the blank with air and then apply a medium CA finish as described on page 58 (**B**).

**9** Wet-sand with the acrylic sanding pads and then buff using the acrylic pen buffing system.

**10** Use a chamfering tool to bevel the inside edge of the pen blank before assembling. If a chamfering tool is not available, an X-Acto knife will suffice. This slight bevel will aid in assembly by guiding the parts into the pen tube without tearing up the plating (**C**).

**11** Assemble your pen blank according to the instructions for the Electra pen kit.

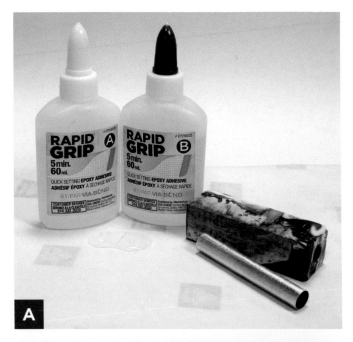

# Gelwriter Classic Click Deer Antler Pen

Turning a biological product such as buffalo horn or antler from deer, elk, antelope, and moose is both rewarding and challenging to the turner. Each antler pen will be unique in its own right because no two antlers are alike.

Working with biological products offers the turner a unique set of challenges. One of the first challenges is the duality of the product. The interior of the antler is soft, and the outer surface is very hard. Drilling antler for pen tubes is easy; however, because the interior is so soft, a liberal amount of CA glue will be needed to ensure a good bond between the antler and the brass pen tube. Another challenge is finding a piece of antler that is straight enough to accommodate the length of the pen tube. Finally, any biological product when sanded, drilled, or turned will emit an odor. Some people will find this odor displeasing. Use adequate ventilation in conjunction with a good dust collection system to assist with the evacuation of the odor.

## Materials

- Gelwriter Classic Click pen kit or kit of your choice
- 7mm adjustable mandrel with classic click bushings
- Deer antler of choice
- Drill bit 8mm
- Pen insertion tool
- Thin and medium cyanoacrylate (CA) glue
- Barrel trimmer or squaring jig
- Pen press
- Sandpaper to 800 grit
- Abralon pads
- Acrylic pen buffing system

**1** Add 1/16" to each end and cut the pen blanks to the proper lengths, using the tubes as guides. Try to find two pieces of antler that are the same size (**A**).

**2** To alleviate the problem of drilling the antler and other irregularly shaped objects off center, use a disc sander to sand flat one or more sides of the blank.

**3** Use a drill vise or pen-drilling vise with an 8mm drill bit and drill a hole through the antler. Glue the pen tubes in using medium CA glue and then square the ends of the blanks using a barrel trimmer (**B**).

**4** Insert an adjustable mandrel into the headstock and place the lower barrel and bushings on the mandrel per the kit instructions.

**5** Because the antler may have an irregular shape, spin the hand wheel before switching on the lathe to ensure that the antler does not strike the tool rest.

**6** Reduce the speed of the lathe to around 600 rpm until the blanks are of uniform roundness. Then, increase the lathe speed to 1800 to 2000 rpm. Only sharp tools will cut the hard exterior of the antler.

**7** Slowly reduce the pen blank to two cylinders using the roughing gouge. Then, using the skew or the Spindlemaster, turn the blanks straight across, leaving them just proud of the bushings. Use a straightedge to check that the antler blank is straight across and does not have any bumps or humps.

**8** Lightly sand the antler using 220 through 800 grit; then, use compressed air to blow off the pen blank. If there are any voids in the blank, fill them with thin CA glue and sand again until smooth (**C**).

**9** Sand through to 800 grit and then use Abralon pads to start the polishing and finishing process. If there are big gaps in the antler, you can fill them with turquoise (**D**).

**10** Use a buffing system with white diamond rouge on a polishing wheel to polish the antler. On the other wheel should be carnauba wax for the final step in the buffing process (**E**).

**11** Line up and assemble all of the parts according to the instructions in the Gelwriter Click-Style Pen kit.

# PROJECT 6
# Inlace Genesis Electra Rollerball Pen

Inlace Acrylester is an acrylic material that can easily be turned and offers a wide variety and assortment of colors. The new Genesis blanks incorporate an organic mesh that is used to structure the blank, giving it a unique look. As with any acrylic, the golden rule applies: taking light bites with sharp tools will give you the best results.

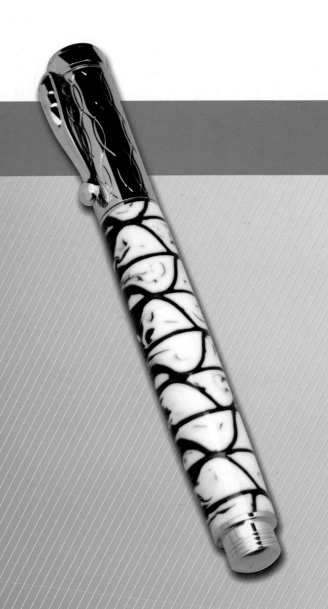

## Materials

- Electra rollerball pen kit or kit of your choice
- Genesis Inlace pen blank or blank of your choice
- 7mm adjustable mandrel with Electra bushings
- Drill bit 10.5mm
- Pen insertion tool
- 5-minute epoxy to glue pen tubes
- Cyanoacrylate (CA) glue, medium, as a finish
- Barrel trimmer or squaring jig
- Pen press
- 320-grit sandpaper
- Acrylic finishing pads
- Acrylic pen buffing system

1   Add ⅛" to each end of the Inlace pen blank and cut the blank to the proper length using the tube as a guide.

2   Drill the blank with a 10.5mm drill bit, relieving the bit often to avoid excess heat buildup and possible blow-out of the blank.

3   Prepare the blank according to Chapter 4, Pen Blank Preparation, page 36.

4   Insert an adjustable mandrel into the headstock and place the front bushing on the mandrel followed by the pen blank (which has not been squared up yet) and then the cap bushing, per the kit instructions.

5   Sharpen your tools before turning any acrylic pen blank. Use a roughing gouge in a bevel rubbing mode lightly touching the blank. Do not be in a hurry to take off too much. Round over the blank and turn it down to just slightly proud of the bushings (**A**).

6   Place the pen blank on the squaring jig and gently square up the blank using a disc sander (**B**). Be careful not to be heavy handed and remove too much of the pen blank! If you did remove too much, on some kits the refill would not completely retract.

7   Place the blank back onto the mandrel and finish turning the blank down to the bushings.

8   When turning acrylics, you do not need to use all the sanding grits. Sand the blank with 320-grit sandpaper to remove any tool marks (**C**). Do not worry about the scratches; they will be removed in the next step by wet-sanding.

9   Wet-sand the blank using the acrylic sanding pads as demonstrated on page 82, then polish and buff using the acrylic pen buffing system (**D**).

10  Use a chamfering tool or X-Acto knife to bevel the inside edge of the pen blank before assembling your pen according to the instructions for the Electra pen kit.

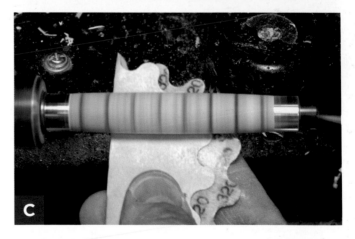

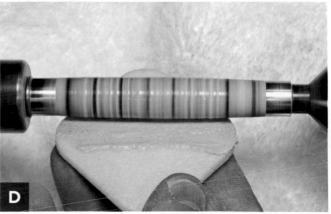

# PART 5

# Turning Advanced Pens

As your skill level increases, you will want to try some different pen kits that have larger-diameter pen tubes, which will make larger pens. You'll also want to incorporate some other advanced skills into your own turnings.

In this section, we will test your skills with a segmented pen from three different exotic woods and turn a closed-end pen with a matching cap finial. I'll also show you how to make a single cross pen, and we'll look at other pen enhancements using plastics and a scroll saw. Laser kits that are cut from wood have exploded in popularity and make it very easy to create custom pens for many applications. Finally, casting your own acrylic pen blanks is becoming more fashionable and will be discussed in detail. Don't be afraid to try something different—you might be surprised by the results!

These pens, from left, feature cigar labels, segmented construction, and laser-cut Stars and Stripes.

# Segmented Pen

Whenever segmented pens are displayed at a show, the comments are always the same: "How did he do that?" or "That man has too much time on his hands!" Making segmented pens is easy and really does not take much more time to create than any other type of pen, but it certainly is more dramatic in appearance. The main consideration is the creating of the pen blank and that is the focus of this segment.

# Materials

- Sterling Silver El Presidente Rollerball Pen kit or kit of choice
- 8mm mandrel (B) with 50B bushings
- Assorted hardwood, preferably contrasting woods
- Masking tape or clear packaging tape
- Planer
- Table saw with ⅛16" blade
- Drill bits, ³¹⁄₆₄" and ³⁵⁄₆₄"
- Drill-centering device
- Spring clamps
- Urethane glue
- Cyanoacrylate (CA) glue, thin and medium
- Disc sander
- Pen press
- Assorted grits of sandpaper through 800 grit and Abralon sanding pads for a soft look
- CA glue for a long-lasting, bright look
- EEE cream and woodturner's finish

The saw blade used for this project is ⅟₁₆" in width and is used because of its narrow kerf. This Diablo 7" narrow-kerf saw blade is readily available.

Choose contrasting woods of lighter and darker colors; for this project, I chose cocobolo, maple, and ebony. By choosing contrasting woods, you will create greater visual impact with your pen.

Plane down your wood so you have a smooth, straight surface for gluing purposes. If you do not have a planer, you can use your table saw as long as you can get a smooth, straight cut.

Commercial pieces of wood are available if a planer is not accessible.

The pen blank will be constructed from cocobolo, ebony, and maple. The final dimensions are ½" x ½" x 8" for the ebony and the maple; the cocobolo is ½" x 1" x 8". Use urethane glue for strength and several spring clamps to clamp the blank together and allow it to dry for at least 8 hours.

Here are a few pen blanks glued up and ready to be cut apart.

**7** Measure the length of the tubes for your particular pen kit.

**8** Let's start with the upper, or the cap, tube. Because the blade in my table saw is 1⁄16" wide, each time a segment of the pen blank is cut, an additional 1⁄16" is also removed. There will be 16 segments in the upper barrel, so that means there will be 16 saw kerfs of 1⁄16" material removed from the pen blank. The overall length of the upper pen barrel will be 2 1⁄16" (pen tube) + 1" for the saw blade kerf for a total length of 3 1⁄16".

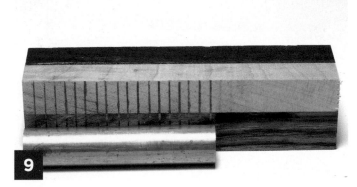

**9** For the lower pen barrel, cut a piece of your glued-up pen blank to 3½" in length using the same calculations you did in Step 8. The lower barrel has an extra ½" on one of the cuts. Trust me, no one ever complained that they were not exactly symmetrical!

**10** Drill the lower barrel with the appropriate drill bit for the pen kit you have chosen using a drill-centering device to ensure that the hole you drill is exactly down the center of the pen blank.

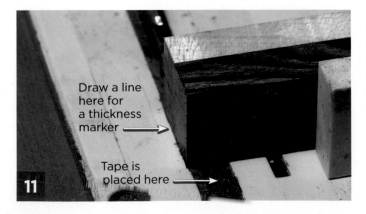

Draw a line here for a thickness marker →

Tape is placed here →

**11**

Place a piece of masking tape or clear packaging tape over the saw blade hole on your table saw to create a zero-tolerance opening (so when you cut the segmented pieces they will not be sucked up into your vacuum system). Place a mark on the packaging tape to show how thick you want to cut the pieces of your pen blank.

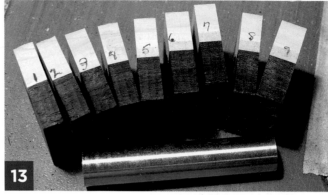

**Caution:** Make sure that, when you start cutting these small segmented pieces, you use proper safety devices to assist you (push sticks and small clamps to hold the pieces). My blade guard has been removed for picture purposes only—do not remove yours!

Cut each piece according to your guidelines in Step 8 and number them as soon as you cut them. This will avoid confusion later when you assemble your piece.

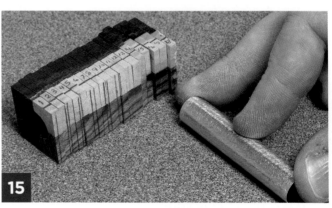

When your sections are cut, draw a reference line on one of the lighter sections of the wood ³⁄₁₆" from one side of the pen blank. This will be used as a reference line when you are assembling your pen blank later. I use ³⁄₁₆" because if you use any thicker line, it will not give a nice flow around the pen.

At this time, scratch the pen tube to prepare for gluing the tube inside the blank.

Lay the segmented pieces flat on a piece of sandpaper and gently sand any tearout that might be there from the saw blade. Also, roll up a piece of sandpaper to fit inside and lightly sand the inside of each segment in preparation for final assembly.

**17**

Take your first two pieces and place a bit of medium CA glue on the two pieces; rub them together to evenly distribute the glue, and then turn them so the reference lines line up with the start of the dark wood. When that is done, place the two pieces on the pen tube, making sure that the tube is flush with the end of wood.

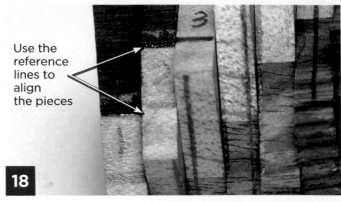

Use the reference lines to align the pieces

**18**

Place a small amount of medium CA glue around the pen tube, and then take the next segmented piece, placing it over the brass tube. Move it back and forth to evenly distribute the glue. Make sure to line up the piece accurately.

**19**

When both barrels are complete, drip thin CA glue over the entire barrel. Let it stand for a few minutes before proceeding to the next step.

**20**

Use a disc sander to sand off the sharp edges of the pen blank. You can do this on the lathe, but be very careful and do not be too aggressive with your cuts; otherwise, you will tear out your pen blank.

**21**

Turn the blank round using the turning tools of your choice.

**22**

When the blank is turned down to the approximate size of the bushings, remove the pen blank from the mandrel and once again drip thin CA glue over the entire pen blank. This may seem like overkill, but because we are working with such small pieces, a little extra care now will prevent a blowout later.

**23**

Continue turning the pen down to the bushings; then, sand to 800 grit and use Abralon pads to finish the pen blank. Follow this step with the finishing method of your choice. For this pen the customer wanted a soft-looking finish so I applied a friction finish using EEE cream and Woodturner's Finish.

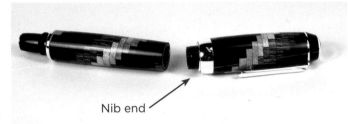

Nib end

**24**

Assemble the cap end per the kit instructions and screw the nib end into the cap.

**25**

Gently insert the lower barrel into the upper barrel, lining up the design. Then, unscrew the lower barrel leaving the nib assembly aligned in the proper orientation. Use a pen press to firmly seat the pieces.

The possibilities for segmented pens are endless. Shown here from top to bottom are three different options: a segmented statesman pen with black titanium plating, the El Presidente pen from the demonstration, and a segmented baron pen with sterling silver plating.

# PROJECT 2
# Closed-End Amboyna Burl Statesman Pen

In the past, the biggest obstacle to making a closed-end pen has been one of holding and turning the blank so it comes out symmetrical. Since the last time we made a closed-end pen in the second edition of the Pen Turner's Workbook, more styles of commercially available closed-end mandrels have been introduced, making it easier for the average pen maker to create a closed-end pen. In this demonstration, we will create a closed-end pen applying a cigar label to the pen with CA glue, and turn a wooden cap finial.

# Materials

- Rhodium 22kt Statesman fountain pen
- Closed-end mandrel
- Over-sized amboyna burl pen blank
- Four-jawed chuck and Jacobs chuck
- Drill Bits—$\frac{37}{64}$", $\frac{15}{32}$", and $\frac{23}{64}$"
- Assorted grits of sandpaper to 800
- Abralon sanding pads
- Medium cyanoacrylate (CA) glue as finish
- Barrel trimmer
- Pen press

PEN PHOTOGRAPH BY SCOTT KRINER

Line up the lower barrel pen parts to assist in measuring the length of the lower barrel. The lower barrel should be long enough to house an ink converter or two ink cartridges.

Measure how deep you will have to drill the lower barrel without going through the other side. For this pen it is 2⅝" deep.

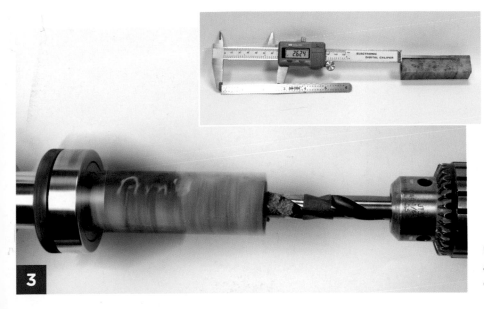

Mark your ¹⁵⁄₃₂" drill bit with some tape at a depth of 2⅝" and drill into the center of the pen blank.

Glue the pen tube into the wood blank and then square the end of the tube using a barrel trimmer with an adapter to fit inside the pen tube.

Closed-end mandrel with bushing and squared up pen blank.

**6**

Place the closed-end mandrel inside the blank and tighten securely. Insert a Jacobs chuck into headstock with the blank on a closed-end mandrel and bring up the tailstock for support.

**7**

Starting with a roughing gouge, use light cuts to reduce the blank, and then use a Spindlemaster or skew to shape the pen until you attain the shape you desire.

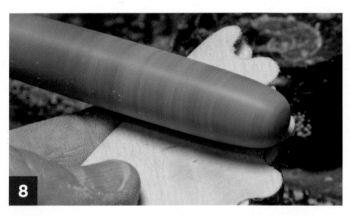

**8**

Sand the blank from 150-grit to 800-grit, followed by the Abralon pads.

**9**

Glue a cigar band to the sanded blank using thin CA glue. Once the label is in place, use many coats of medium CA glue to thoroughly cover the cigar band.

**10**

Use 320-grit sandpaper to remove any glue ridges and smooth the medium CA glue.

**11**

Wet-sand the CA glue finish and then polish and buff.

**12**

If you choose to make a wooden cap finial, then follow Steps 11 to 18: Insert a piece of wood approximately 1¾" into a four-jawed chuck and reduce the piece to make a tenon that will fit inside the brass tube on the cap end of the pen. **Caution:** Because this is a small piece, your hands will be close to the spinning chuck.

**13**

Use a spare upper barrel pen tube as a gauge to test fit the tenon. The brass tube should fit snugly over the tenon. Make sure you cut a square shoulder on the tenon so the barrel will fit snugly against it.

**14**

Insert a Jacobs chuck in the tailstock and drill a ²³⁄₆₄" hole into the tenon to accommodate the nib of the pen.

**15**

Turn the upper barrel as per the kit instructions and sand to 800-grit followed by Abralon pads. Remove the upper barrel and test-fit it onto the cap finial, making sure the finial is flush with the upper barrel and fits snugly. Finish sanding through to the Abralon pads with both pieces fitting together.

**16**

Cut the finial off the block of wood, reverse it, and place it into a spare brass tube for an upper barrel so that the top of the finial can be turned, sanded, and finished with CA glue.

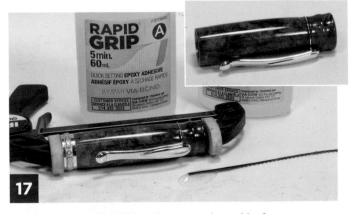

**17**

Dry-fit the cap finial into the upper barrel before you glue it in. Scratch the inside of the upper barrel tube with some sandpaper and place a small amount of 5-minute epoxy around the cap finial to glue it into the upper barrel.

# Single Cross Pen

Making cross pens usually gets the same response as the segmented pen: "He's got too much time on his hands!" Trust me, I don't! These pens are very good sellers at the upscale pen shows because no one else is taking the time to make them. Yes, it does take a little extra time to prepare the pen blank, but the results are dramatic and they all sell! So, take the plunge and turn a pen or two, and you will be rewarded for your efforts!

# Materials

- Sterling Silver Churchill Fountain Pen kit or kit of choice
- 8mm precision mandrel (B) with 16B bushings
- ⅞" x ⅞" x 5" cocobolo or pen blank of choice
- ⅛" ash wood or other light contrasting wood for accent striping material
- Drill bits, ³¹⁄₆₄" and ³³⁄₆₄"
- Cyanoacrylate (CA) glue, thin and medium
- Disc sander
- Pen press
- Assorted grits of sandpaper through 800 grit and Abralon sanding pads for a soft satin look
- EEE cream and woodturner's finish

**1** If you are going to make a lot of cross pens, some sort of cutting jig will be a very handy item. If not, a disc sander may be used to get a flush side on which to glue the accent stripe.

**2** Cut the upper and lower halves of the pen blanks using the pen tubes as a guide.

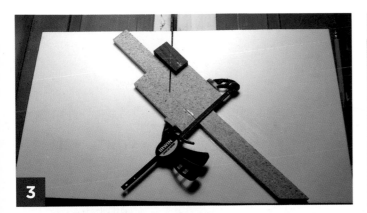

**3** Place the upper barrel on the cutting jig and adjust the sliding block to the center of the pen blank. Mark the lower portion of the pen blank with an arrow for orientation. The bottom of the blank with the arrow side will always be placed in the corner when cutting the blank.

**4** Then, cut the upper barrel, as indicated.

**5** Glue a ⅛" piece of accent wood into the cut halves of the blank using medium CA glue. Then, place the pen blank arrow side down into the cutting jig and cut the other side of the cross.

**6** Glue another ⅛" piece of accent wood onto the other cut half of the blank using medium CA glue. **Hint:** Glue one half at a time; trying to glue two slippery sides together is hard to accomplish.

Once the other ⅛" stripe is glued into the blank, sand the edges flush with a disc sander.

Drip thin CA glue over the entire blank to add strength to the blank. Then, once the glue has dried, drill exactly through the center of the blank.

Drip thin CA glue down the inside of the blank for additional strength. Complete the same task for the lower barrel as well, and then glue the pen tubes inside the blanks using medium CA glue.

Taking light cuts to avoid chipping out the blanks, turn the blank until you get close to the bushings. Place more thin CA glue on the cross sections.

Complete the turning, sanding, and finishing processes. The crosses should line up and cross in the center of one another.

# Helpful Hints for Assembly of the Single Cross Pen

Once you have finished your single cross pen, you'll want to assemble it so that the crosses are aligned. Here are some helpful hints for getting everything to line up just right. (I used a single cross pen turned from Corian as an example.)

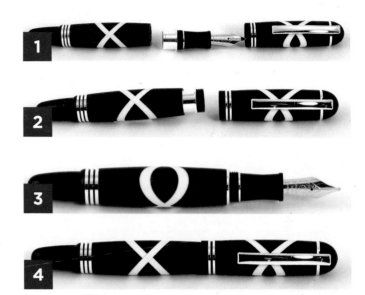

1. Line up the parts for assembly with the crosses facing up. Then, screw the nib into the nib coupler and gently push it into the cap, making sure the crosses line up.

2. Gently unscrew the top barrel from the lower barrel, ensuring the nib coupler remains in the same position.

3. Press the nib coupler into the final position in the lower barrel and screw the nib into the nib coupler.

4. Final Corian single cross pen.

# OTHER PEN ENHANCERS

Inserting .010" plastic pieces into your work for accent stripes will add some life to your project.

Cut apart your pen blank using a scroll saw or a band saw.

Insert a few of the plastic pen enhancers into the cut pen blanks and glue the pieces together using medium CA glue and spring clamps.

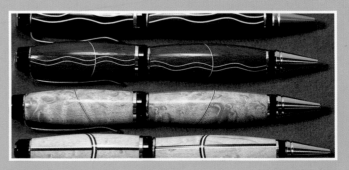

Here are some examples of the plastic pen enhancers glued into several different pens.

# PROJECT 4
# Laser Pen Kits

Before lasers, a scroll saw or a band saw was used to cut wavy lines in pens. A scroll saw can cut very intricate lines better than a band saw, but neither can compare to the accuracy of a laser. Consequently, laser engravers have opened up new frontiers for pen turners. One vendor, Kallenshaan Woods, is putting together custom pen kits for the pen turning market. The problem with laser engraving companies is that the lasers are expensive to own, so they must produce item after item to pay for the upkeep; therefore, engraving companies are not willing to experiment on different techniques. Kallenshaan was willing to experiment and as a result has adapted rotary attachments to obtain the precision cuts needed to make the kits for pen turners.

This Stars & Stripes pen was made for the former Speaker of the U. S. House of Representatives, Rep. Dennis Hastert. Since making that pen for him, I have made many stars-and-stripes pens for other national and local politicians. This project will focus on creating the pen blank for the pen rather than on the turning and assembly of the actual pen.

## Materials

- Tycoon rhodium pen kit
- 7mm mandrel with Tycoon bushings
- Thin and medium cyanoacrylate (CA) glue
- Hobby knife
- Black acrylic paint
- Pen insertion tool
- Squaring jig & disc sander
- Pen press
- Assorted sandpaper from 150–800
- Abralon pads
- Acrylic finishing pads
- Acrylic pen buffing system

**1** Open and inspect the kit to see that it contains all of the parts. Carefully remove the stars from the star board and turn them so the darker (laser-burned) side is facing up. Rough up pen tubes and paint them with black acrylic paint.

**2** The stars are tapered—insert the smaller part into the hole for a better fit.

**3** Insert the painted upper pen tube into the star field but do not glue it in at this time. Use the sharp point of a hobby knife to lightly stab the stars and insert them into the holes.

**4** Use the shank of the hobby knife to apply pressure to push the stars into the holes.

**5** When all the stars have been seated and the pen tube is centered inside the star field, use a pen insertion tool and drip thin CA glue all over the entire pen. The CA glue will penetrate and secure the pen tube inside the blank.

**6** The stripes come as a cage with the stripes already assembled. Insert the painted lower pen tube into the blank.

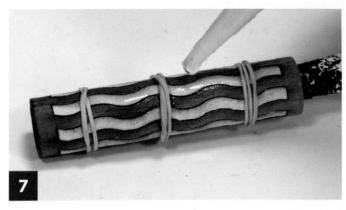

**7**

Once the painted pen tube is centered properly, drip thin CA glue all over the entire blank—if there were any gaps, the black painted pen tube would not show any voids.

**8**

Do not use a barrel trimmer on this blank—it would tear up the stripes!

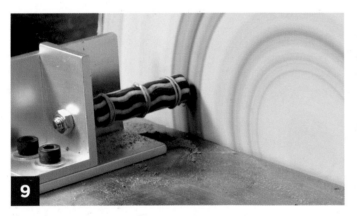

**9**

Use a squaring jig on the disk sander to square the ends of the pen blanks.

**10**

Use a Spindlemaster or skew to give final shape to the pen. If you are apprehensive about using any turning tools, you may sand the blank with 80-grit sandpaper to get it down to the bushings.

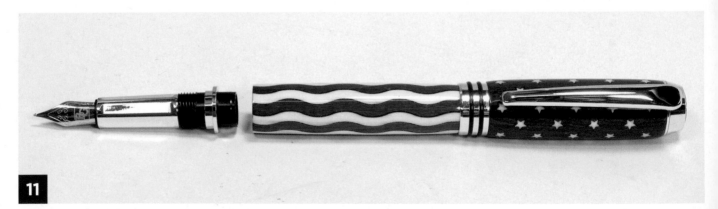

**11**

After the CA glue finish is applied, assemble the pen as per kit instructions. When making a fountain pen, make sure that you align the pen nib with the clip of the pen.

# PROJECT 5

# Casting Clear Acrylic Pen Blanks

The biggest myth about casting is that you need a pressure pot to cast pen blanks. You do not need a pressure pot to make nice pen blanks! I have been making award-winning pens for years without using a pressure pot. What you need to do is take your time and when the blanks are in the mold, roll the blanks around to let any bubbles that did form come to the surface. Coating pen tubes with clear resin to make your own unique pens is not new and this project will offer some insight and suggestions on how to accomplish this task with ease. When creating these masterpieces, your imagination is your only limiting factor. A number of different items can be placed on a pen tube and then coated with acrylic. For example, though you are certainly not limited to the following items:

Stamps, beer caps, snakeskin, wrapping paper, abalone shell pieces, pigmy seahorses, tiny starfish, smokeless tobacco tins, watch parts, surgical scalpels, scrapbook pieces, small crystals, photographs; or, have an artist paint the pen tubes or paint them yourself.

You can place anything on the pen tube and coat it with clear acrylic as long as no item sticks up so high that, when the pen is covered with acrylic and turned down to the bushings, it breaks through the acrylic.

## Materials

- Sierra Vista rhodium pen kit
- 7mm mandrel with Sierra Vista bushings
- Thin and medium cyanoacrylate (CA) glue
- Acrylic paint
- Pen insertion tool
- Squaring jig & disc sander
- Pen press
- 320-grit sandpaper
- Acrylic finishing pads
- Acrylic pen buffing system

Inspect the contents of the casting kit to ensure all items are included.

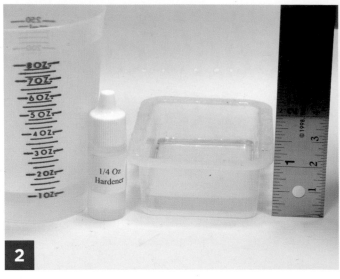

To 1 ounce of casting acrylic, add 6 drops of hardener and mix thoroughly; then, pour into the mold to approximately ³⁄₁₆" to ¼" in depth. Allow this to dry overnight.

A casting pot is not needed to obtain bubble free pen blanks.

These are just some items that can be easily adhered to the pen tube when making your own casted pen blanks.

While the first pour of the casting resin is drying, prepare the tubes that will go into the mold. Use acrylic paint from a craft store and paint the background of the pen tube.

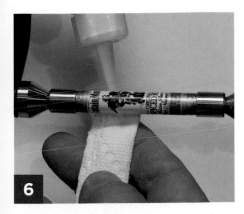

**6** Use thin CA glue to adhere a label to the painted tube.

**7** Medium CA glue is used to glue the starfish and miniature seahorses to the painted pen tube.

**8** Here are #22 fly fishing lures glued to the pen tube using medium CA glue.

**9** Abalone shell pieces can be glued onto the painted tube with medium CA glue.

**10** Once you have prepared the tubes, place a suitable rubber stopper in one end of the tube and then pour the copper ball-bearing weights into the tube to weight it. Place the other stopper into the other end of the tube.

**11** Place the weighted pen tubes into the mold on top of the first layer of resin. Measure another 1 ounce of resin, mix it with hardener, and pour it over top of the tubes. Fill the mold deep enough to cover half to three-quarters of the pen tubes. If you filled it up to the top you would risk getting air bubbles. Use a wooden craft stick to roll the pen tubes around and remove any air bubbles.

**12** After the second layer has hardened (usually overnight), measure another 1 ounce of resin with the appropriate amount of hardener and pour it over the entire mold.

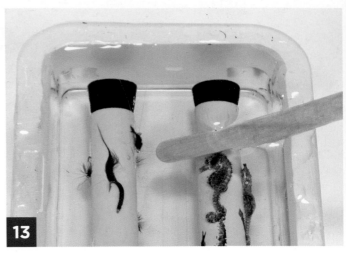

**13** Once again use a craft stick to remove any air bubbles you may happen to see.

**14**

Let the resin cure overnight and once it is completely dry, turn the mold upside and twist it until the resin pops out. The mold can be used many times if it is not broken.

**15** Cut the mold apart, remove the rubber plugs and save the weights to be used over again.

**16** Use a barrel trimmer or squaring jig to square the ends of the pen tube. Mount it on the mandrel and start to turn your cast blank. Remember the golden rule of acrylics: "Sharp tools and light bites."

Continue turning the pen blank down to the bushings and use a skew as a scraper to take small bites of material off at a time as you get close to the bushings.

Use a piece of 320 grit sandpaper to remove any tool marks you might have in your pen blank.

Wet-sand the blank using the acrylic finishing pads followed by a drop of scratch remover.

Polish and buff using the acrylic pen buffing system to remove all micro-scratches and then assemble your pen blank according to the kit instructions.

Blowouts

Misalignments

Cracks

Visible glue joints

Chips

# PART 6

# FAQs and Troubleshooting

"A dumb question is one that is not asked." That is my opening statement to my students. In the next few pages, I will share some of my bloopers and blunders to demonstrate that we all make mistakes. I hope you will learn from my mistakes and not make as many yourself. Remember, we all make mistakes. However, as you become more skilled as a turner, these little mistakes will become a distant memory of days past.

If you look closely at this photo, you'll find common flaws in pen-making, and in the pages that follow, you'll find good solutions for avoiding or repairing these flaws.

**Question: How can I keep the brass tube from showing through on some of my acrylic pens?**

**Answer:** To keep the brass tube from showing through an acrylic pen, paint the brass tube before you glue it into the acrylic pen blank. You can use acrylic craft paint or any metal spray paint, such as Rustoleum. Scratch the tube first so the paint will stick, and then paint the tube a color similar to the acrylic pen blank.

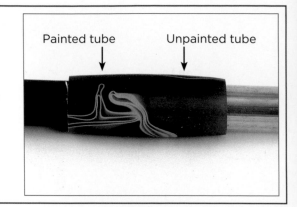

Painted tube    Unpainted tube

**Question: How do I remove my glued finger from my pen blank?**

**Answer:** CA glue does not discriminate between wood and your fingers. Use the utmost care when gluing because contact with your skin can cause serious injury. Use CA glue solvent, nail polish remover, or acetone to remove the glue from your finger and the pen blank.

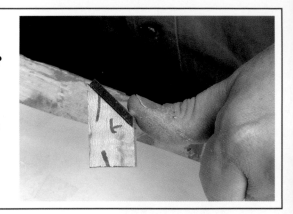

**Question: How do I keep the ends of my pen blank from splitting when I use the barrel trimmer?**

**Answer:** Keep the barrel trimmer sharp and do not put excessive force on the pen blank when you're trying to square it. Take light cuts, and/or use a squaring jig as shown below.

**Question: How and why do I have to square the ends of my pen barrel?**

**Answer:** The pen barrel ends have to be perpendicular to the mandrel. If they are not, you will have a difficult time assembling the pen parts. You can use a barrel trimmer as demonstrated in the slimline pen project (see page 55) or you can use a disc sander and a squaring jig, as shown.

**Question: Can I sharpen a barrel trimmer?**

**Answer:** Yes. Remove the cutting head and end. Use a diamond hone to lightly file each flute, keeping the same angle that is currently on the cutting head.

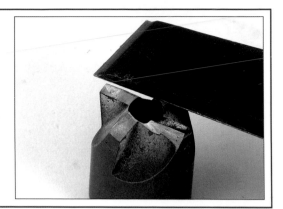

**Question: How do I prevent the pen blank from blowing out when I drill it?**

**Answer:** Slow down the speed on the drill press and relieve the chips often while drilling. You can cut the pen tube slightly longer, and as the bit starts to come through, stop the drilling and then cut the end with a scroll saw or a band saw. Also, you may place a scrap piece of wood on the bottom of the blank and drill directly into that. Most important: use a sharp bit and relieve the debris often.

**Question: How do I get the hole in my pen blank?**
**Answer:** Use a drill press and a drill-centering device (see page 37 in Chapter 4, "Pen Blank Preparation").

**Question: Why did my pen crack after one week?**
**Answer:** This usually occurs when green wood (not dried wood) is used. To prevent this, use kiln-dried lumber or stabilized pen blanks (see page 25 in Chapter 2, "Selecting Materials").

**Question: Where can I purchase pen kits, and who makes the best pen kits?**
**Answer:** Pen kits may be purchased from a variety of sources. As far as who makes the best ones, that is a matter of personal choice for a particular pen style and plating.

**Question: Do all pen bushings fit all mandrels?**
**Answer:** No, mandrels come in two sizes: 7mm, or A, mandrels, and 8mm, or B, mandrels. The bushings are designed for a particular kit and will only fit either the 7mm or the 8mm mandrel (see Figure 1.17 on page 16).

**Question: What is the best finish to put on a wood pen?**
**Answer:** Everyone has his own method of finishing a pen. My two finishing methods, which are shown throughout this book, are fast, simple, and hold up over time. However, please experiment on your own to find what works best for you (see Project 1, Slimline Pen, on page 59)!

**Question: How do I tighten the loose wooden finial cap on my closed-end pen?**

**Answer:** Place a small amount of thin CA glue on the tenon and spread it around the entire circumference to fill any gaps and to build up some girth. Sand lightly to ensure a good fit.

**Question: What do I do if the nib with the converter attached is too long to fit inside the lower pen barrel?**

**Answer:** Carefully drill the inside of the barrel with a ¼" drill bit until the converter fits.

**Question: How can I get a few more seconds out of the CA glue when I'm gluing the tubes?**

**Answer:** Using medium CA glue will allow you a few extra seconds to coat the inside of the pen blank; however, it still must be done quickly to avoid the pen tube's being glued into the blank prematurely. If you are having problems with CA glue, try 5-minute epoxy. It will give you much more working time, especially with wet or green wood.

**Question: Why is my finished pen not round? (Or when the pen is in the open position, the top is not aligned and the entire pen is out of round.)**

**Answer:** The tailstock and/or the locking nut are too tight, which may cause the mandrel to be slightly out of round. This will not be apparent until the pen is assembled. Also, too much tool pressure may have been applied.

**Question: How can I avoid tearout when I'm working with non-stabilized wood, or "punky" wood?**

**Answer:** Place some thin CA glue right into the punky area of the wood to harden the material so it can be turned easily.

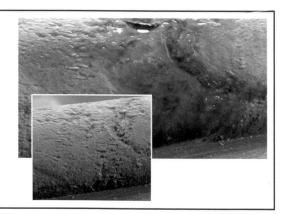

**Question: What do I do if my acrylic material splits and cracks?**

**Answer:** Reduce the acrylic material slowly. If you are too aggressive, you may damage the pen blank beyond repair. Remember, light, easy cuts with sharp tools work best. You can always take more material off, but you cannot put it back on! If you are having trouble when initially rounding the blank, sand the edges off before turning on the lathe.

**Question: How do I fix a ballpoint that sticks out past the pen tip on a cigar-style pen when the pen is in the closed position?**

**Answer:** Unscrew the twist mechanism until the ballpoint tip retracts inside the tip housing. Measure the space and make a spacer using plastic thick enough to fill this void.

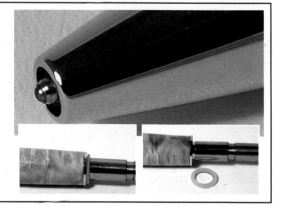

**Question: How can I get rid of glue that is left inside the pen tube even after the barrel trimmer is used?**

**Answer:** Use a hobby knife to remove excess glue within the pen tube.

**Question: Can I fix cracks or large pieces that chip off the pen blank?**

**Answer:** There are two ways to repair the cracks and chips. The first is to glue the big piece back into the blank using medium CA glue. The second way is to use ground-up shavings, and then glue them back into the torn area. Compare the two and you will see the difference: The ground-up shavings look better because you cannot see the glue joint.

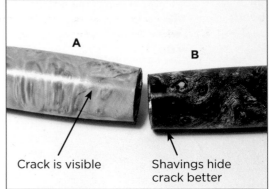

Crack is visible

Shavings hide crack better

**A**

**B**

**Question: Is there anything I can do about a blemish on the upper barrel portion of the pen?**

**Answer:** Hide the blemish under the clip.

Blemish

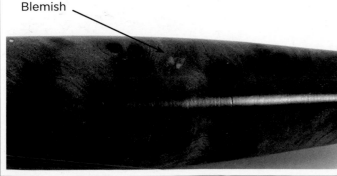

**Question: I placed the twist mechanism too deep in the lower barrel. Now when the pen is closed, the refill sticks out of the pen tip. How do I fix it?**

**Answer:** Disassemble the pen with a dissassembly kit (see the Disassembling a Pen sidebar below).

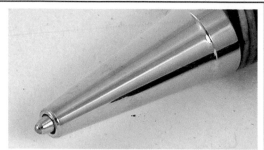

# DISASSEMBLING A PEN

1 Remove the pen refill and replace it with the thin rod. Hold the lower barrel and gently tap the thin rod until the tip is removed.

2 Insert the twist mechanism into the retainer.

3 Place the thicker rod into the retainer, and then place this into a vise or a pen press and push the twist mechanism out into the retainer.

4 Here is your disassembled pen.

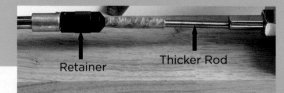

Retainer        Thicker Rod

# PART 7

# Marketing

As I said in the beginning of this book, life is too short to own an ugly pen! Be proud of your creation. Show your pens to everyone and tell them you made that pen, and people will always say, "Really... you made that?" I cannot tell you how many pens I have sold just by letting people know that I made a pen by hand.

So, now that you have made this hand-crafted, one-of-a-kind, stunning, impressive, fine writing instrument, what do you do with it? Giving it to your mother who appreciates anything you give her may be gratifying at first, but how many pens can she really use? Now that each member of your family and all of your friends have six pens, it may be time to think about selling your work. But how exactly do you do that?

There are entire books devoted to how to market and sell your wooden creations. Therefore, this section is by no means going to give you the silver bullet step-by-step key to success. However, it will offer some realistic ideas on how to sell your pens, display your work at shows, photograph your creations, present your pens to your customers, price your work, and set realistic expectations based on your turnings.

All kidding aside, this is probably the most important section of this book. Whether you are making pens with the specific objective of starting your own business or just to sell them to earn extra money, the first rule is to be realistic. In all probability, you will not take an order for 1,000 pens your first week. The following information should give you some general guidelines for marketing your work.

### Wholesale Versus Retail

Ask yourself, do you want to sell your pens directly to the public or do you want to have a shop owner sell them for you? Selling retail to the public directly is hard work. You will need to obtain a tax number to collect sales tax, a store of some kind (actual or virtual via the Internet), and many other items best addressed by a book on the business of selling.

Selling your pens wholesale to a gallery or craft shop will alleviate some of the problems associated with directly selling to the public. There are advantages to selling wholesale; however, you do have to find the right store that will sell both you as the artist and your work, but, more importantly, one that will pay you in a timely fashion for what is sold.

If you acquire a large-quantity order, batch your work, completing one part of the process at a time. These wine stopper corkscrew blanks were all squared at one time.

With production work, turn as many pieces as you can on a mandrel at one time. Here, one complete wine stopper and another half are being turned at the same time.

### Production Work

When you acquire your first large-quantity order for pens or other turnings, euphoria is your first feeling, followed by "what did I get myself into," closely followed by fear. You immediately start to question yourself: Did I price the item correctly? Can I deliver them on time? What if they do not like them? These and other questions will surely dance through your head, but have no fear. You have read this book and will have all the answers!

Production work is just that: boring. You make the same item over and over again. One suggestion is to do everything at one time. Glue all of the blanks at one time, followed by drilling them all at once. Complete each task and then move on to the next. When you are turning them, if you can place an extra piece of work on the mandrel, by all means do it.

### Finding a Market for Your Work

I have been a sales manager for over 35 years with experience in training sales representatives how to "sell." The first objective that is stressed for any good sales representative is to listen. We have two ears and one mouth, so why do we talk twice as much as we listen? Listen to what your customer is telling you.

The only way for you to find out what the public wants is to conduct your own market research. I can make suggestions but you will be the one selling your work. Visit the galleries and local shops to find out what the public is purchasing. If you like a particular pen style such as a Slimline and you ask the shop owner if they sell any Slimline pens and they tell you that they do not sell them, then you have your answer to what the public wants or, in this case doesn't want. Do your homework!

### Finding the Correct Location

How do you find the right store? Again, ask questions. How long have they been in business? What is their customer profile? Are their customers affluent? Is the store you are thinking about part of a large mall or is it a stand-alone shop? These are questions that you are entitled to ask. After all, you do want your work to be sold and, more importantly, want to get paid for it, don't you?

When you are in the store, look around. See the quality of the other merchandise being offered and look at the prices. Is this in the range where you want to sell your work? I personally place all of my pens in "upscale" affluent shops. Here, I know that the patrons can afford the price I want to charge for my pens.

Another rule of mine is that I will not put my pens in a store that does not sell pens. I want competition. I want the customers to see the other craftsmanship, compare it to mine, and see the quality they get when they purchase my pen!

## Getting Established

A good way to establish yourself is to offer your work for local fundraising. The local ambulance squad was having a fundraiser, and I offered to split the proceeds of the sales of my pens as a donation to the ambulance squad. This accomplished three things. First, it was good to give to the ambulance squad by donating the profits to charity. Second, it established my work in the area and exposed me to many people that I would not have met because the fundraiser was held in a large mall. And third, as a result, many other orders were taken for special pens to be delivered at a later time.

## Local Festivals, Craft Shows, and Specific Fountain Pen Shows

There are many different types of shows: juried craft shows, art festivals, local craft shows, and flea markets. I personally choose the higher-end juried craft shows and festivals. A juried show means that a panel of judges will look over representative digital images of your work and grade them. The artists with the highest scores will be

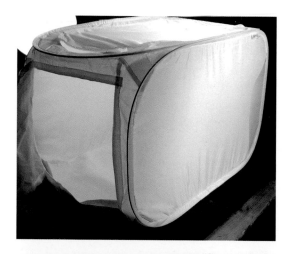

Lights on the sides and top of this commercial pop-up photo tent evenly distribute light and remove any shadows.

This homemade photo tent was made using ¼" threaded rod blocks of wood with a drapery liner thrown over the top.

granted admission to the show. These types of shows will boast that "more than 2,000 artists applied and only 175 gifted artists were chosen," making you feel special to be selected! Juried shows usually will charge the public an admission fee whereas local craft shows are generally free to the public. When the public is charged admission to the show, they know that the work they will see will be of higher quality than a local craft show because the work has been reviewed by a judging panel.

Before you can become a vendor at a juried show, you will have to send digital images of your work. In addition, you will have to show an image of your booth to ensure that the booth meets their standards. Make sure your images are good quality, well lighted, and representative of your work.

## Displaying Your Work

The key is proper lighting! I will say it again—lighting. Use high-intensity lighting and some sort of stair-step display to raise your work to eye level. Other venders at shows have walked from the other side of the room with a pen or watch just to see their product under my lighting. Lighting makes your work pop with brilliance. However, good lighting can be a double-edged sword if your pens are not finished properly: the customer can see flaws in your work. Be careful to inspect what your customers expect.

Accept credit cards and let people know this. A friend of mine at another show did not accept credit cards, and people walked from his booth to mine just because I accepted them. Finally, have a writing tablet with good-quality ink available for people to try your fountain pens.

## Displays for Shows and Booth Etiquette

Your booth set-up can be something simple for a table display, or an elaborate booth for an indoor high-end show. You are the only one who knows what type of audience you will have at the show. For a quick tabletop display, purchase 6" x 12" cardboard boxes from an office supply store and then cover them with table covers to form stair steps. I do this when I travel to the Los Angeles pen show. For outdoor shows (some offer electricity, some do not), I have a pop-up tent with 6' tables and table covers, and my stair-step display of wood. For the higher-end indoor shows, I have made my displays from wooden shelves from IKEA and placed lights under each shelf for maximum lighting.

Booth etiquette is important and each one of you is saying, "Yes, I know what to say and how to act"; however, I see so many violations that I must state the obvious once

Use stands with high intensity lighting to illuminate your work. Have a writing tablet with good-quality paper and ink so customers can try your pens.

This tent and sun shade keeps me and my pens dry and safe at outdoor shows.

Dramatic under-shelf lighting transforms these discount-store units into high-quality displays.

more: Do not sit and text or talk on the phone when someone is in your booth! You are telling them that they are not important. You have paid good money to be at this show. Put the phone away and greet your customer and show them you are interested in them!

## Customizing Your Fine Writing Instruments

When presenting your pens, each pen should carry a brief printed description of the material, how you created the pen, and any other interesting fact about the pen. Customers want to know how you do things and the more they are educated, they more likely they will purchase from you.

This is where a laser engraving company can make or break a sale for you by helping you create something different for your customer.

How are you packaging your pens? Are you just showing them in a display case that holds a number of pens, or are you offering individual customized boxes for each particular pen? There is a plethora of pen boxes on the market, but the more ornate the box is, the better your chance of selling to the customer.

You can send your wooden boxes to a laser engraving company and have them further customize your pen boxes to specifically match your pens, as I did at the beginning of this chapter.

## Pricing Your Work

I have saved the best for last! The first rule and the best rule of selling, I truly believe, is placing a value on your time and sticking with it. How much should I charge for my pens? If I had a buck for every time I heard that, I would not have to write this book! The old adage—time is money—works here, too. Your time has a value. If someone picks up your pen and says that is too much money, do not argue. I tell them that they are right and that my pen is not for them. I am proud of my work, and I am not ashamed to charge for it!

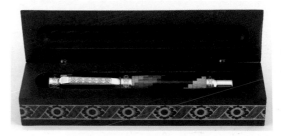

A customized box will enhance a pen's value.

Printed tags inside the presentation cases tell my customers about their beautiful pen.

# Index

Note: Page numbers in italics indicate projects.